The
PASSION
according
to
G.H.

Emergent Literatures

Jacques Godbout, **An American Story**
Adrienne Kennedy, **In One Act**
Gerald Vizenor, **The Trickster of Liberty**

The
PASSION
according
to

Clarice LISPECTOR

Translation by
**Ronald W.
SOUSA**

University of Minnesota Press
Minneapolis

Published by the University of Minnesota Press
111 Third Avenue South, Suite 290, Minneapolis, MN 55401-2520
Published simultaneously in Canada
by Fitzhenry & Whiteside Limited, Markham.
Printed in the United States of America on acid-free paper.

Third printing, 1997

Library of Congress Cataloging-in-Publication Data

Lispector, Clarice.
   The passion according to G.H.
   (Emergent Literature)
   Translation of: A paixão sequndo G.H.
   I. Title.   II. Series.
PQ9697.L585P313   1988   869.3   88-4763
ISBN 0-8166-1711-2
ISBN 0-8166-1712-0 (pbk.)

The University of Minnesota
is an equal-opportunity
educator and employer.

To Potential Readers:

This is a book just like any other book. But I would be happy if it were read only by people whose outlook is fully formed. People who know that an approach—to anything whatsoever—must be carried out gradually and laboriously, that it must traverse even the very opposite of what is being approached. They and they alone will, slowly, come to understand that this book exacts nothing of anyone. Over time, the character G. H. came to give *me*, for example, a very difficult pleasure; but it *is* called pleasure.

C. L.

A complete life may be one ending in so full identification with the non-self that there is no self to die.

Bernard Berenson

ONCE
within a
ROOM

Ronald W. SOUSA

When a woman known to us simply as G. H. enters a room
that "nominally" belongs to her, she experiences the frus-
trations of many of the expectations normally associated
with a room. This room seemingly refuses to play the role
of a static container, takes on a living force of its own, and
virtually comes to impose itself upon its "owner." As the
room expands and contracts, G. H.'s identity is continually
undone and remade through the progress of her narration.

As this scenario suggests, the story of G. H. does
not fulfill the expectations we commonly bring to a narrative. In effect, it breaks down several of our "containers" or
categories that serve to render the world comprehensible.

The most important of those containers, as far as the
translator and the reader of *The Passion According to G.
H.* are concerned, are those touching on literary concerns.
The fact that the Ukraine-born Clarice Lispector (1924-
1977) became a literary *cause-célèbre* in her adopted Brazil
but is viewed in France, because of the very same texts, as
an important contemporary philosopher dealing with the
relationships between language and human (especially
female) subjecthood says much about the genre problem-
atic. Are we to take G.H.'s story as fiction or as speculation

on philosophical problems in and through the narration of what we would traditionally call a "plot"? Where does literature end and philosophy begin? Intellectually speaking, that question is an easy one to answer: they both end in "language," which for Lispector is the medium within which such designations as "literature" and "philosophy" are made, as well as the medium in and through which alone anything nonlinguistic can be reached. The problem is that for her language is also fallacious unless it is pushed to its limits and thereby made to reveal what, in its structuring as a container, it seeks to hide.

Because of that exploration of language, *The Passion According to G. H.* comprises a series of nontraditional language usages. It is constituted by segments somewhat but not wholly linearly arranged. They are in fact repetitive, with additions and deletions in each new installment—with, then, both movement and return; and with every successive movement comes reelaboration of already established issues in radically different ways. The text also comprises: inconsistencies in punctuation practice; juxtaposition of colloquial phrases, poetic phrases, and phrases that are completely non-Portuguese; creation of fictitious allusions; reuse of apparently important terms with slightly changed signification, seemingly to avoid creation of consistent terminology; wholesale, but not therefore meaningless, violations of traditional grammar and syntax, and of the concepts of association and exclusion that underlie them; and employment of complex verbal-conceptual ambiguities. A prominent example of the last of those practices is to be seen in the word "passion," which in Portuguese is the colloquial term for "love" and "lover," in addition to its designation of "passion" as an abstraction and of Christ's Passion. Since it is completely undecidable whether the "the" of the book's title should be translated, that title could just as easily be rendered "Love According to G. H." as it could with the formulation I have given it, which emphasizes the Biblical implications also invoked.

As a translator preparing this singular text for a reading public unable to go to the original, I have felt acutely the ways in which traditional expectations have been violated, for such violation has robbed me of useful ways of structuring my presentation. What I have done as a result is to treat the Portuguese original in quite specific ways. (The original used is the second edition, Rio de Janeiro, Editôra Sabiá Ltda., 1968; although acknowledgment of the fact is nowhere made, it was substantially revised from the copyright-dated first edition, Rio de Janeiro Editôra do Autor, 1964.) I have subordinated the rendition of many of what would traditionally be called "literary devices" to delineation, first and foremost, of the intellectual positions set forth in the book, and only thereafter have I endeavored to reproduce such features as style variation and artful use — or violation — of language norms. In so doing, I have often made the translated text more conventional than the original, regularly had to paraphrase where no single term was readily available in English, and occasionally had recourse to philosophical terminology where the original uses more ambiguous, and therefore more powerful, formulations. The result is a text that has lost something of the ambiguity and idiosyncrasy that is part and parcel of the original from which it arises and has become more expository in tone than that original. I invite the reader to imagine a Portuguese text that transmits a much greater sense of potential language chaos than does the translation.

This result may or may not be called "translation," but then that undecidability is only fitting in regard to a work that may or may not be called a "novel."

R. S.
1988

The
PASSION
according
to
G.H.

I keep looking, looking. Trying to understand. Trying to give what I have gone through to someone else, and I don't know who, but I don't want to be alone with that experience. I don't know what to do with it, I'm terrified of that profound disorganization. I'm not sure I even believe in what happened to me. Did something happen, and did I, because I didn't know how to experience it, end up experiencing something else instead? It's that something that I'd like to call disorganization, and then I'd have the confidence to venture forth because I would know where to come back to: to the prior organization. I prefer to call it disorganization because I don't want to ground myself in what I experienced—in that grounding I would lose the world as it was for me before, and I know that I don't have the capacity for another one.

If I go ahead with that grounding and consider myself true, I'll be lost because I won't know where to set up my new way of being—if I go ahead with my fragmentary visions, the whole world will have to change for me to fit into it.

Something's missing that once was essential to me

and is so no longer. I don't need it anymore, as though I had lost a third leg that until then kept me from walking but made me a stable tripod. It's that third leg that's now missing. And I've gone back to being someone I never was. I've gone back to having something I never had before: just my two legs. I know that I can walk only when I have two legs. But I sense the irrelevant loss of the third one, and it horrifies me, it was that leg that made me able to find myself, and without even having to look.

Am I disorganized because I have lost something I didn't even need? In this new cowardice of mine—cowardice is what has happened to me most recently, my greatest adventure, it is so wide a field that only great courage enables me to accept it—in my new cowardice, which is like waking up in the morning in a stranger's house, I don't know if I'll have the courage simply to set out. It's hard to lose oneself. So hard that I'll probably soon work out a way of finding myself, even if finding myself is again the lie that I live on. Up to now, finding myself was having a ready-made person-idea and mounting myself inside it: I incarnated myself inside that set-up person and didn't even sense the great construction project that living was. The person-idea that I had came from that third leg of mine, the one that held me fast to the ground. But now . . . will I be freer?

No! I know that I'm still not sensing freely, that once again I'm thinking because my goal is to find—and that for safety's sake I'll call the moment that I come across a way out "finding." Why don't I have the courage to find just a way in? Oh, I know that I *have* gone in. But I've been afraid because I don't know where that way in leads. And I've never before let myself go without knowing where.

Yesterday, however, I lost my human constitution for hours and hours. If I'm brave, I'll let myself stay lost. But I'm afraid of new things and I'm afraid to experience what I don't understand—I always want the guarantee of at least thinking that I understand, I don't know how to just give myself over to disorientation. How do I explain that my greatest fear is precisely in relation to . . . to being? and that there is nonetheless no other way to go. How to explain that my greatest fear is precisely the fear of having to live out whatever happens? how to explain that I cannot bear to look out, only because life is not at all what I thought it was and is in fact something other—as though I had known before what it was! Why is it that just looking is so greatly disorganizing?

And disillusioning too. But what could I become disillusioned about? if I was barely able to stand my merely constructed organization without at least sensing? Maybe disillusionment is the fear of no longer fitting into a system? It could, however, be said that he is very happy who finally experiences disillusionment. What I was before wasn't good for me. But it was from that ungood that I put together something better: I had put together hope. From my own ungood I had created a future good. Am I now afraid that my new outlook won't make sense? But why don't I just let myself be guided by whatever happens? I shall have to run the holy risk of chance. And replace fate with probability.

But are the discoveries of infancy like those made in a laboratory, where one finds what one will? Was it, then, only when I became an adult that I started to fear and grew the third leg? Can I, as an adult, have the childlike courage to lose myself? to lose oneself is to go looking with no sense of what to do with what you might find. The two walking feet minus that extra third one that holds a person down. And I want to be held down. I don't know what to do with the horrifying freedom that can destroy me. But while I was held down, was I happy? Or was there—and there was—an uncanny, restless something in my happy prison routine? Or was there—and there was—that throbbing something to which I was so accustomed that I thought throbbing was the same as being a person? Isn't that it? yes, that too . . . that too . . .

I become so scared when I realize that over a period of hours I lost my human constitution. I don't know if I'll have another one to replace the lost one with. I know that I'll need to take care not to surreptitiously use a new third leg that can grow back in me as easily as a weed, and then call that protective leg "a truth."

But I also don't know what form to give to what happened to me. And for me nothing exists unless I give it a form. And . . . and what if the reality is precisely that nothing has existed?! maybe nothing happened to me? I can understand only what happens to me, but only what I understand happens . . . what do I know about the rest? the rest hasn't existed. Maybe nothing has existed! Maybe I have merely undergone a great, slow disintegration. And my struggle against that disintegration is just that: is just trying to give it a form. A form gives contours to chaos, gives a construct to amorphous substance . . . the vision of an infinite flesh is a madman's vision, but if I cut that flesh into pieces and spread those pieces over days and famines . . . then it will no longer be perdition and madness: it will be humanized life again.

Humanized life. I had humanized life too much.

But what shall I do now? Shall I hold onto the whole vision, even though it means holding onto an incomprehensible truth? or shall I give form to nothingness and let that be my way of integrating my very disintegration into myself? But I am so poorly prepared to understand. Before, whenever I tried, my limitations gave me a sensation of physical discomfort, in me, any effort to think immediately runs up against my head. Early on I had to recognize coldly the obstacle that my meager intelligence represented and reject setting out on any path. I knew that it was my fate to think little, reasoning power kept me fast inside my own skin. How, then, could I now start thinking? and maybe only thought could save me, I'm afraid of passion.

Now that I have to save tomorrow, that I have to have a form because I don't sense that I have the strength to stay disorganized, now that, fatefully, I shall have to frame that monstrous, infinite flesh and cut it into pieces that something the size of my mouth can take in, and the size of my eyes' vision, now that I shall fatefully succumb to the necessity of form that comes from my fear of being undelimited—then let me at least have the courage to let that form form by itself, like a crust that hardens on its own, a fiery nebula that cools into earth. And let me have the great courage to resist the temptation to invent a form.

The effort that I shall now make to let a sense, whatever it may be, rise to the surface, that effort could be made easier if I pretended to write for someone.

But I'm afraid to start writing to be understood by that imaginary someone, I'm afraid I'll start "making" a sense, with the same meek madness that up to yesterday was my "healthy" way of fitting into a system. Will I have to have the courage to use an undefended heart and go on speaking to nothing and no one? as when a child thinks about nothingness. And to run the risk of being crushed by chance.

I don't understand what I saw. I don't even know if I saw it, since my eyes ended up not being separate from what I saw. Only in an unexpected rippling of the lines, only in an anomaly in the uninterrupted continuity of my culture, did I for an instant experience life-giving death. That purified death that made me sort through the forbidden weft of life. Saying the name of life is forbidden. And I almost said it. I almost couldn't disentangle myself from its weft, which would have been the destruction of my age inside me.

Perhaps what happened to me is an understanding . . . and for me to be true, I have to continue being separate from it, have to continue not understanding it. All sudden understanding very closely approximates a clear nonunderstanding.

No. All sudden understanding is in the last analysis the revelation of a clear nonunderstanding. Every moment of finding is the losing of oneself. Perhaps I experienced an understanding that was as complete as an ignoring, and I shall emerge from it as intact and innocent as before. Any comprehension on my part will never be equal to that understanding, for I can reach only the height of living — the only level on which I function is the level of living. Only now, now I know of a secret. Which I am already forgetting; oh I feel that I am already forgetting . . .

To rediscover it now I would have to die all over again. And knowing it again could be the murder of my human soul. And I don't want to, I don't want to. What could still save me would be for me to deliver myself over to that new ignorance; that would be possible. For all the while that I am struggling to know, my new ignorance, which is forgetting, has become sacred. I am the priestess of a secret that I no longer know. And I serve out of blissful ignorance. I found out something I was unable to understand, my lips became sealed, and I retained only the incomprehensible fragments of a ritual. Although for the first time I feel that my forgetting is, in the last analysis, of a piece with the world. Oh, and I don't want in the least to have anything explained to me that would have to be made to go beyond itself to be explained. I don't want anything explained to me that would require human validation again for its interpretation.

Life and death have been mine, and I was a monstrosity. Mine was the courage of the sleepwalker who simply acts. During those hours of perdition, I had the courage neither to compose nor to organize. And especially the courage not to look ahead. Up to then I had not been brave enough to let myself be guided by what I don't know toward what I don't know: my foresight preconditioned what I would see. It wasn't the foresight of seeing: it already had my care's dimensions about it. My foresight closed the world to me.

Until, for a few hours, I stopped. And, my God, I got what I didn't want. It wasn't a river valley I walked along—I had always imagined that discovery would be fertile and humid, like river valleys. I never thought it would be the immense disencounter that it was.

Is my sacrifice for continuing to be human just forgetting? I shall now be able to recognize in the common faces of some people that . . . that they have forgotten. And that they no longer know that they have forgotten what they have forgotten.

I saw it. I know I did because I didn't give it its meaning. I know that I did because I don't understand it. I know I did because what I saw isn't good for anything. Listen, I'm going to have to talk because I don't know what to do with that moment of living that I experienced. Worse yet: I don't like what I saw. It explodes my day-to-day life. I apologize for putting this all on you, I would have much preferred seeing something better. Take what I experienced, free me from my useless vision, from my useless sin.

I'm so frightened that I shall be able to accept the notion that I have lost myself only if I imagine that someone is holding my hand.

Putting my hand in someone else's has always been my definition of happiness. Before I fall asleep, often—in that small struggle not to lose consciousness and go into the greater world—often, before I get up the courage to go into the vastness of sleep, I pretend that someone has my hand in theirs, and then I go, go to that enormous absence of form that is sleep. And when even after that I don't have courage, I dream.

Going to sleep is very much like the way that I now have of going to my freedom. Giving myself over to something I don't understand is placing myself on the brink of nothingness. It is going just by going, like a blindwoman lost in a field. That supernatural thing that is living. The living that I had tamed and made familiar. That courageous thing that is for me to give myself over and is like reaching out a hand to God's ghostly hand and entering that formless thing that is a paradise. A paradise that I don't want!

During the time I'm writing and speaking, I'm going to have to pretend that someone is holding my hand.

Oh, at least at the beginning . . . only at the beginning. As soon as I can do without it, I'll go on alone. In the meantime, I need to hold this hand of yours—even if I can't picture your face and your eyes and your mouth. But even though it is cut off from a body, this hand doesn't scare me. Its creation comes from an idea of love such that it is as if the hand were really attached to a body, and if I don't see it it's because I am unable to love more. I'm not up to picturing a whole person because I'm not a whole person myself. And how can I imagine a face if I don't know what kind of expression I need on it? As soon as I can get along without your warm hand, I'll go on alone—and in terror. That terror will be my responsibility until the metamorphosis is complete and the terror is transformed into clarity. Not the clarity born of a desire for beauty and morality like the kind I looked for before even without knowing it, but rather the natural clarity of what exists, and it is that natural clarity that terrifies me. Even though I know that the terror . . . the terror is only myself coming face to face with things.

In the meantime, I am inventing your presence, just as one day I shall also be unable to let myself die alone, dying is the greatest peril of all, I won't be able to pass over into death and put my first foot into my first self-absence — in that last and so first an hour too I shall invent your name-less presence and with you I shall start to die until I am able on my own not to exist, and then I'll let you go. For now, I have you, and your warm, unknown life is my only internal organization, I who without your hand would feel unat-tached within the enormous space that I have discovered. The space of truth?

But the fact is that truth has never made sense to me. Truth doesn't make sense! That's why I was afraid of it, and still am. Forsaken as I am, I give everything over to you — so you can do something pleasant with it. If I talk to you will I frighten you and lose you? but if I don't, I'll lose myself and in losing myself lose you anyhow

Truth doesn't make sense, the hugeness of the world makes me shrink. What I probably asked for and finally found still ended up leaving me unprepared, like a child walking alone across the earth. So unprepared that only my love of all the universe could console me and sat-isfy me, only a love such that the very egg-cell of things would resonate with what I call love. With what in fact I am merely naming without knowing its name.

Could it have been love that I saw? But what kind of love is it that is as blind as an egg-cell? is that what it was? that terror, was it . . . love? a love so neutral that — no, I don't want to talk to myself anymore, to talk would be to precipitate a sense just like making yourself suddenly stable with the paralyzing security of that third leg. Or am I simply putting off starting to talk? why am I saying nothing and just playing for time? Because I'm afraid. I need courage to go forth with an attempt to concretize what I feel. It's as though I possessed a coin and didn't know what country it was good in.

I shall need courage to do what I'm going to do: to talk. And to run the risk of the enormous surprise that I am going to feel at the poverty of what I say. As soon as I say it, I'll have to add: "That isn't it, that isn't it at all!" But I'll also need not to be afraid of being foolish, I've always gone for the less rather than the more for fear of seeming foolish along the way: and also there's the wounding of one's dignity. I'm putting off the moment when I have to talk. Is it because I'm afraid?

And because I don't have a word to say.

I don't have a word to say. Why don't I just stay quiet, then? But if I don't force myself to talk, silence will forever engulf me in waves. Word and form will be the plank on top of which I shall float over billows of silence.

And if I keep putting off starting, it's also because I have no guide. Other travelers' accounts give me few facts about the trip: all their information is horribly incomplete.

I feel that an incipient freedom is gradually taking me over. . . . For never before today have I had so little fear of lacking good taste: I just wrote "billows of silence," which I wouldn't have said before because I have always respected beauty and its intrinsic decorum. I have said "billows of silence," my heart humbly bows, and I accept it. Have I in effect abandoned a whole system of good taste? But is that my only gain? How imprisoned I must have been that I feel myself freer just because I no longer fear a lack of aesthetics. . . . I still don't foresee what else I may have gained. Maybe I'll learn of it little by little. For now, the first timid pleasure that I feel is being able to say that I have lost my fear of the ugly. And that loss is a very great good. It is a delight.

I want to know what more I've gained by losing. As of now, I don't know: only in reliving it will I experience it.

But how can I relive it? If I don't have a normal word to say. Shall I have to make words as though I were creating what happened to me?

I am going to create what happened to me. Only because living isn't tellable. Living isn't livable. I shall have to create upon life. And without lying. Yes to creation, no to lying. Creation isn't imagination, it's running the huge risk of coming face to face with reality. Understanding is a creation, it's my only way. I shall have to painstakingly translate telegraph signals—translate the unknown into a language that I don't know, and not even understand what the signals amount to. I shall speak in that sleep-walker's language that if I were awake wouldn't even be a language.

And I'll create the truth of what happened to me. Oh, it will be more a graphism than a writing, since I shall be engaging in reproduction rather than expression. I need to express myself less all the time. Have I lost that as well? No, even when I did sculpture I was only reproducing, and only with my hands.

Will I stay lost amid the silence of the signals? I will, for I know what I'm like: I never learned to look without needing more than just to see. I know that I'll terrify myself like someone who was blind and then finally opened her eyes and saw—but saw what? a mute, incomprehensible triangle. Couldn't that person consider herself blinder still for seeing only an incomprehensible triangle?

I ask myself: if·I look into the darkness with a magnifying glass, will I see more than darkness? the glass won't disperse the darkness, it will only reveal it all the more. And if I look at brightness with a magnifying glass, I shall see, with a shock, only greater brightness. I have seen but am as blind as before because I saw an incomprehensible triangle. Unless I also transform myself into a triangle that will see in the incomprehensible triangle my own source and repetition.

I'm stalling. I know that everything I say is just to put it off—to put off the moment when I'll have to start talking, knowing that there is nothing more for me to say. I'm putting off my silence. Have I been putting off silence for my whole life? but now, in my disparagement of the word, perhaps I'll finally be able to start talking.

The telegraph signals. The world bristling with antennas, and here am I receiving the signal. I'll be able to do only a phonetic transcription. Three thousand years ago I lost my head, and all that was left were phonetic fragments of me. I'm blinder than before. I did see, I really did. And I was terrified by the raw truth of a world whose greatest horror is that it is so alive that for me to admit that I am as alive as it is—and my most hideous discovery is that I am as alive as it is—I shall have to raise my consciousness of life outside to so high a point that it would amount to a crime against my personal life.

For the profound morality that I felt before—my morality was the desire to understand, and, since I didn't understand, I shuffled things around, that was only yesterday, and now that I discover that I have always been profoundly moral: I admit only of finality—as for my prior profound morality, for me to discover that I am as crudely alive as that bare light that I learned of yesterday, as for that morality of mine, the harsh glory of being alive is horror itself. I lived before of a humanized world; did the simply alive destroy the morality that I had then?

A world wholly alive has a Hellish power.

A world wholly alive has a Hellish power.

Yesterday morning—when I went out of the dining room to the maid's room—I had no way of knowing that I was but a step away from discovering an empire. Just a step away. My more primary struggle for more primary life was about to open with the calm, voracious ferocity of desert animals. I was about to confront within myself a degree of living so originary that it bordered on the inanimate. Nothing I was doing, however, gave any hint that I, my lips dry with thirst, was going to begin to exist.

It was only afterward that an old phrase would occur to me, one that years before I had foolishly engraved in my memory, just the subtitle of a magazine article that I ended up not reading: "Lost in the Fiery Hell of a Canyon a Woman Desperately Struggles for Life." I had no way of foreseeing where I was headed. But then I never was able to see how things were leaning; every time they reached a culmination, it always seemed to me to be a surprising rupture, an abrupt explosion, at a specific moment, and not the continuation of an uninterrupted flow.

That morning, before I went into the maid's room, what was I? I was what others had always seen me as, and that was the way I knew myself. I don't know how to explain what I was. But at least I want to remember: what was I doing?

It was almost ten in the morning, and it had been a long time since my apartment had been so much my own. The maid had quit the day before. The fact that there was no one talking or walking around and making something happen magnified with its silence this dwelling in which I live in my semiluxury. I was lingering at the coffee table—how hard it is becoming to know what I was like. But I have to make the effort to at least give myself a prior form, so I can understand what happened when I lost that form.

I was lingering over the coffee table, making little balls out of the center of the bread—is that right? I need to know, I need to know what I was like! This is how I was: I was distractedly making little, round balls out of the heart of the bread, and my last, tranquil, amorous liaison had dissolved amicably, with a caress, and I had again come into the happy and lightly insipid pleasure of freedom. Does that situate me? I am pleasant, I have sincere friendships, and my awareness of that gives me a gladsome friendship with myself that has never excluded a certain self-directed irony, albeit one that I don't push very far.

But . . . what that silence of mine was like before I don't know and have never discovered. Sometimes, while looking at a snapshot taken at the beach or at a party, I would notice, with a slight, ironic apprehension, what that smiling, dimmed face showed about me: a silence. A silence and a destiny that were escaping me, me a hieroglyphic fragment of an empire living or dead. Looking at the picture I could see the mystery. No. I'm going to lose the rest of my fear of bad taste, I'm going to start my exercise in courage, living isn't courage, knowing that you're living, that's courage—and I swear that in the photograph of me I

could see the Mystery. I would be taken slightly by surprise, it's only now that I am discovering that it was a surprise: in those smiling eyes there was a silence such as I have
seen only in lakes and heard only in silence itself.

Never, then, did I have reason to think that one day
I would go to encounter that silence. To encounter the
splintering of silence. I would take a quick glance at the face
in the photograph and, for a second, in that inexpressive
face the world would look equally inexpressively back at
me. Was that—just that—my closest contact with myself?
the greatest silent sounding I have attained, my blindest,
most direct link with the world. The rest . . . the rest
amounted to various organizations of myself, I know that
now, oh now I know. The rest was how I had transformed
myself little by little into the person who bears my name.
And I ended up being my name. All you need to do is see
the initials G. H. in the leather of my luggage to know that
that's me. And I have never demanded of anyone else anything more than the mere coverage of the initials of their
names. What is more, "psychology" has never held any
interest for me. I used to become impatient, and still do,
with the psychological attitude; it's an instrument that
simply transcends. I think I left the psychological stage
behind with adolescence.

G. H. had lived a great deal, that is, had experienced many facts. Have I somehow perhaps been in a hurry
to experience everything I would have to experience as soon
as possible, so that I would have extra time to . . . to live
without facts? to *live*. Did I early on discharge all my sense
duties—early and quickly experience pains and pleasures—to get free all the sooner of my lesser human destiny? to get free so that I could seek my tragedy.

My tragedy lay somewhere. Where was my greater
destiny? one that wasn't just the plot of my life. The trag-

photo = abyss

edy—which is the greater adventure—had never taken place in me. My personal destiny was all I knew. And all I wanted to know.

I spread about me a tranquility that comes from my having reached a certain degree of realization about what it means to be G. H., even on luggage. Also, without reflection, I have adopted my reputation for my so-called inner life: I treat myself as others treat me, I am what others see in me. When I was alone there was no fall-off, there was merely one degree less of what I was like with the others, and that was always my naturalness and my health. And my brand of beauty. Was it only my photographs that pictured an abyss? an abyss.

An abyss of nothingness. Just that huge, empty thing: abyss.

I act like what is referred to as a finished person. Intermittent sculpting over an indeterminate period of time also gave me a past and a present that allowed others to situate me: they allude to me as someone who does sculptures that wouldn't be bad if they were less amateurish. For a woman, that reputation is a great thing socially and it has located me, as much for myself as for others, in an area between man and woman, socially speaking. Which left me much freer to be a woman, since I was making no formal effort to be one.

As regards my so-called inner life, perhaps it was the sporadic sculpting that has given it a slight tone of pre-climax—perhaps because of that certain kind of attentiveness that even dilettantish art brings with it. Or because I have had the experience of patiently clearing away material to find gradually its immanent sculpture; or because, again from the sculpture, I have suffered the enforced objectivity of struggling with something that was other than myself.

All this has given me the slight tone of preclimax characteristic of someone who knows that, if I listen attentively to objects, something of those objects will come forth and be imparted to me that will then in turn be given back to the objects. Maybe it was that tone of preclimax that I saw in the smiling, ghostly photograph of a face whose voice is an inexpressive silence, all people's pictures are portraits of the Mona Lisa.

And is that all I can say about myself? That I'm "sincere"? I am, more or less. I don't lie to conjure up false truths. But I have used truths as a pretext too much. Truth as a pretext for lying? I could just tell myself things that flattered me and then tell the underside. But I have to be careful not to confuse defects with truths. I am afraid of what being sincere would lead me to: to my so-called nobility, which I pass over, to my so-called vulgarity, with which I do likewise. The more sincere I might become, the more I'll be led to flatter myself, both with my occasional nobilities and especially with my occasional vulgarity. The only thing sincerity doesn't lead me to do is pride myself on my inconsequentiality. That I leave out altogether and not just for lack of self-pardon, I who have pardoned every great and important thing in myself. Inconsequentiality I omit because confession is often a point of vanity for me, even painful confession.

It isn't that I want to be pure of vanity, but I need to clear myself from the field to be able to move in it. If I can move. Or is wanting not to be subject to vanity the worst form of vanity itself? No, I think I just need to be able to look without having the color of my eyes matter. I need to get rid of myself to be able to see.

And is that all I was? When I open my door to unexpected visitors, what I glimpse in the faces of the people who see me at the door is that they have just glimpsed in me my tender preclimax. What the others get from me is, then, reflected back to form the atmosphere of what is called "me." That preclimax may have been my whole existence up to now. The other—anonymous and unknown— that other existence of mine that was merely profound was what probably gave me the sense of security of a person who always has the kettle on a low flame in the kitchen: whatever occasion might arise, I'd always have water boiling.

Only the water had never boiled. I didn't need violence, I just bubbled about enough to keep the water from ever boiling and overflowing. No, I haven't known violence. I was born without a mission, my nature didn't impart one to me; and I have always had a light enough hand not to impress a role upon myself. I didn't give myself a role, but I did organize myself for the purposes of my own understanding. I couldn't put up with not finding myself in the catalog. My question, if I had one, wasn't "what am I?" but rather "among whom am I?" My cycle was complete: what I was experiencing in the present had already been conditioned in such a way that I could understand myself as a result. An eye looked over my life. I probably called that eye sometimes "truth," sometimes morality, sometimes human law, sometimes "God," sometimes "myself." For the most part I lived inside a mirror. Two minutes after I was born I had already lost my beginnings.

A step away from the climax, a step away from the revolution, a step away from what is called love. A step away from my life—which, because of a kind of strong reverse magnet, I wasn't making into a life; and also because of a will to order. Life's disorder is bad taste. And even I wouldn't have known how to transform that latent step away into a real step if I had wanted to. Because of pleasure in a harmonious coherence, because of the greedy, ever-promising pleasure of holding and not having to put out—I didn't need the climax, the revolution, or even that prelove that is so much happier than love itself. [Was the promise all I needed? Yes, just a promise)

Maybe that attitude—or lack of attitude—also came from the fact that never having married or borne children I haven't, so to speak, had to wear any shackles, or break any: I've been continuously free. Being continuously free has been helped along by my facile nature: I eat and drink and sleep facile. And of course my freedom has also come from my financial independence.

I suppose my habit of thinking only at the moment when it is necessary came from my sculpture, for it taught me to think only with my hands and only at the time of using them. Also from my intermittent sculpting came my habit of pleasure, to which I already tended by nature: my eyes had handled the form of things so much that I became more and more accustomed to pleasure and rooted myself in it. I could, with much less than my whole self, I could work with anything: just like yesterday at the coffee table, where all I needed to form round forms from the bread heart was the surface of my fingers and the surface of the bread. To do what I could do I had never needed either suffering or talent. What I had in my power wasn't for me a conquest, it was a natural gift.

And among women and men, what was I? I have always had an extremely tender admiration for male habits and ways of doing things and take an unurgent pleasure in being female, being female was also a natural gift for me. I've only had a facility for such gifts and not the awe of any vocation—I think that's it, isn't it?

From the table over which I was lingering because I had time, I looked around, while my fingers were making the bread heart into balls. The world was a strange place.

Which allowed me to live: in the world I could stick one little ball of bread heart to another, I just needed to put one beside the other and then all I had to do was push them together, with very little effort, just enough for one surface to adhere to the other, that way, pleasurefully, I was making a curious pyramid that gave me pleasure: a right triangle made of round forms, a form made up of forms opposite to itself. If that had any meaning for me, the bread heart and my fingers probably knew what it was.

The apartment reflects me. It's on the top floor, which is considered elegant. People in my circle try to live in the so-called penthouse. It's more than elegant. It's a real pleasure: you can command a city from up here. When that elegance becomes common, will I, without even thinking why, move to another kind of elegance? Maybe. Just like me, the apartment has moist lights and shadows, nothing here is sharp: one room precedes and anticipates the next. From my dining room I could see the mixture of shadows that formed a prelude to the living room. Everything here is the elegant, ironic, witty riposte of a life that has never existed anywhere: my home is merely an artistic creation.

In fact, everything here refers to a life that ⌊if it were real, would little serve me. What does it trace out, then? If it were real, I wouldn't understand it, but I enjoy the copy and understand it.⌋ The copy is very pretty. The circle of artistic and semiartistic people that I live in should, however, make me disdain copies; but I have always seemed to prefer parody, it has served me well. Tracing a life probably gave me—or does it still? to what extent has the harmony of my past life exploded?—tracing a life probably gave me a sense of security precisely because the life wasn't mine: it wasn't a responsibility that I had to deal with.

The slight, generalized pleasure—which seems to have been the tone in which I live, or lived—has perhaps come from the fact that the world was neither me nor mine: I could take pleasure in it. Just as I had not made men mine either and could therefore admire and sincerely love them, as one loves nonegotistically, as one loves an idea. Since they were not mine, I never tortured them.

As one loves an idea. My home's witty elegance comes from the fact that everything here is in quotation marks. To be honest about true authorship, I cite the world, I have repeatedly cited it, since it was neither me nor mine. Was beauty, a certain kind of beauty, my object, as it is for everyone? did I live in beauty?

As for myself, without either lying or telling the truth—just as in that moment yesterday morning when I was sitting at the coffee table—as for myself, I have always kept one quotation mark to my left and another to my right. In a certain sense, "as if it wasn't me" was wider than if it was—a nonexistent life completely possessed me, occupied me like an invention. Only in the photograph, when the negative was developed, was there something else developed as well—something which, not accomplished by me, was accomplished by the snapshot: when the negative was printed it showed my ectoplasmic presence. Is photography the portrait of a concavity, of a lack, of an absence?

All the while I was, more than just clean and correct, I was a pretty riposte. For all that is probably what makes me pretty and generous. A man of experience has only to glance at me to tell that here is a woman of grace and generosity, one who is no bother, who doesn't tear a man down: a woman who smiles and laughs. I respect others' pleasure, and I take my own pleasure delicately, tedium nourishes me and delicately consumes me, the sweet tedium of a honeymoon.

That image of myself between quotation marks used to satisfy me, and not just superficially. I was the image of what I wasn't, and that image of my nonbeing fulfilled me entirely: one of the strongest ways of being is to be negatively. Since I didn't know what I was, "nonbeing" was my closest approximation to truth: at least I controlled the flip side: I at least had the "non," I had my opposite. What was good for me I didn't then know; I experienced, with some pre-fervor, what was bad for me.

And in experiencing that "bad," I experienced the backside of what I couldn't even try to want or to attempt. Just like someone who leads a life of "depravity" with peril and love and at least has the opposite of what she neither knows nor wants nor can achieve: the life of a nun. Only now do I know that I had everything in my hands, though in a backward way: I was dedicating myself to every detail on the 'non' side. Through nonbeing in detail, I proved to myself that—that I was.

That manner of nonbeing was much more pleasant, much cleaner: for, with no irony now, I am a woman of spirit. And of spirited body. At the coffee table, I was framing myself in my white robe, my clean, well-sculpted face, and my simple body. From me there irradiated the kind of dignity that comes from indulgence in one's own pleasures and in others' pleasures. I was delicately consuming my own and delicately wiping my mouth with the napkin.

That her, G. H. in the luggage leather, was me; is it . . . still? No! Hence I calculate that the hardest thing my vanity will have to face will be my own judgment: I shall have all the appearance of one who has experienced failure, and only I shall know if it was requisite failure.

Only I shall know if it was requisite failure.

I arose at last from the coffee table, that woman. Since there was no maid that day, I would be engaging in the sort of activity I liked most: cleaning up. I've always liked putting things in their places. I think it's my only true calling. <u>By ordering things I create</u> and understand at the same time. But since, through reasonably well-placed investments, I have gradually become pretty well-off, I've been kept from putting that calling into practice: if I hadn't belonged to the class that I do by reason of both money and culture, I would normally have had a domestic's job in some rich people's great house, where there is a great deal to put in order. Ordering is finding the best form. If I had been a domestic like that, I wouldn't even have needed my dilettantish sculpture; if I could have liberally ordered with my hands. Ordered form itself?

I found the ever-forbidden pleasure of putting a house in order so great that even while I sat at the table, I had already begun to take pleasure in the mere planning of it. I looked out around the apartment: where should I start?

Also because afterward, at the seventh hour, just as on the seventh day, I'd be free to rest and have the remainder of a day in repose. Repose almost without joy, which would be a good balance for me: from my hours of sculpture I had learned almost joyless calm. I had enjoyed myself too much the last week, had gone out too much, had had too much of whatever I wanted, and I now wanted the day to be exactly as it promised to be: toilsome and empty and good. I would make it go as long as possible.

Maybe I'd start by organizing the back of the apartment: the maid's room was probably filthy, what with its dual function of sleeping quarters and storeroom for old suitcases and clothes, back newspapers, leftover wrapping paper and string. I'd get it clean and ready for the new maid. Then, from that end of the apartment, I would progress slowly, "climbing" horizontally to the opposite end, the living room, where—as though I myself were the finishing point of the cleaning and of the morning—I would stretch out on the sofa and read the newspaper, probably drowsing in the process. If the telephone didn't ring.

With that in mind, I decided to take the phone off the hook, to be sure that I wouldn't be bothered by anything.

How can I now explain that at that very moment I had begun to see something that would become clear only later? without knowing it I was now in the antechamber of the room. I had begun to see and I didn't know it; I had seen since I was born and I didn't yet know it, I didn't know it.

Give me your anonymous hand, for life is giving me pain and I don't know how to go on talking—reality is too delicate, only reality is delicate, my unreality and my imagination are more substantial.

Having decided to start my ordering in the maid's room, I went through the kitchen, which leads to the service area. At the end of the service area the hallway starts that leads to the maid's room. Before going on, however, I leaned against the wall in the service area to finish smoking my cigarette.

I looked down: thirteen floors of building below. I didn't know that all of it was already playing a part in what was going to happen. The process had probably begun a thousand times before and had then been led astray. This time it would go all the way to its end, and I didn't foresee it at all.

I looked at the inside area, the backs of all the apartments, for which my own apartment too existed as a back. On the outside, my building was white, with the smoothness of marble and the smoothness of finished surface. But on the inside, the inside area was a chaotic jumble of square blocks, windows, dark streaks and blotches from the rain, window snarling at window, mouths looking into mouths. My building's mass was like a factory's. The miniature of a vast landscape of passages and canyons: smoking there, as though on a mountaintop, I looked out over the view, probably with the same inexpressive gaze that could be seen in the photographs of me.

I saw what all of that expressed: it all expressed nothing. And I took in that nothing with great attentiveness, took it in with what was in my eyes in those pictures; only now do I know that I was continuously receiving that silent signal. I looked down at the inside area. All of it had an inanimate richness about it that recalled the richness of nature itself: here you could also prospect for uranium and from here oil could gush forth.

I was seeing what only later would I feel—I mean, only later would I experience a profound loss of meaning. Only later would I understand: what seems a lack of meaning . . . is what meaning there is. Every instant of "lack of meaning" is precisely the frightening certainty that it is there that meaning lies and that I not only can't reach it but don't want to because there are no guarantees. Only later would the lack of meaning besiege me. Could a sense of the lack of meaning have always been my negative mode of sensing meaning? it had been my participation.

What I was seeing in the monstrous, machine insides that was the inside area of my building, what I was seeing were things that had been made, eminently practical things with practical purposes.

But something of terrible, general nature—which I would later experience within myself—something of fateful nature had fatefully come forth from the hands of the hundred practical workmen who had installed water and drainpipes, wholly unaware that they were constructing this Egyptian ruin at which I was now staring with the stare that was in the photographs of me on the beach. Only later would I know that I had seen: only later, after seeing the secret, did I realize that I had already seen it.

I tossed the lighted cigarette over the edge and took a step back, slyly hoping that no neighbor would link me to that act prohibited by the Building Management. After a moment, I carefully stuck my head out and looked down: I couldn't even tell where the cigarette had landed. The precipice had silently swallowed it up. Was I thinking then? at least I was thinking about nothing. Or maybe about the possibility that some neighbor had seen me commit that forbidden act, which didn't go at all with the cultured woman that I was pictured as being, which made me smile.

Then I went up the dark hallway that leads to the service area.

I went up the dark hallway that leads to the service area.

In that hallway, which forms the very back of the apartment, two doors face each other, indistinct in the shadows: the service exit and the door to the maid's quarters. The outback of my home. I opened the door to the expectation of stacks of newspapers and a dark pile of storage and junk.

But as I opened the door, I had to squint in reaction and in physical revulsion.

Instead of the jumbled shadows that I was expecting, I encountered the vision of a room that was a quadrangle of white light; my eyes squinted in self-protection.

For the past almost six months — the length of time that maid had been with me — I had not ventured in there, and my astonishment came from finding a completely clean room.

I had expected to find dark corners, I had prepared myself to have to throw the window wide open and bathe musty darkness with fresh air. What I hadn't expected was that the maid, without saying anything to me, had fixed the room up the way she wanted it, and, acting as though she owned it herself, had done away with its function as a storage area.

From the doorway I now looked in on a room that had about it a calm, empty order. Without telling me, the maid had opened up a dry, empty space in my fresh, cozy, moist home. What I had now was a room that was completely clean and shiny, like a room in an insane asylum from which all dangerous objects have been removed.

Here, now, because of the space that had been created, were concentrated the reverberations from the roofs, from the cement terraces, from the erect antennae of all the neighboring buildings, from the reflections of a thousand building windows. The room seemed to occupy a level much higher than that of the rest of the apartment.

Like a minaret. My first impression of a minaret began with this room: free-floating above a limitless expanse. At the time, I perceived only my physical discomfort with that impression.

The sides of the room weren't uniform: two of the angles were slightly greater than square. And while that was its physical reality, it descended upon me as though it was my own vision that was deforming it. It seemed like a paper representation of how I might perceive a four-sided figure: already deformed in its lines of perspective. The concretization of a flaw in vision, the materialization of an optical illusion. Its not being entirely regular in its angles gave it an appearance of basic fragility, as though this minaret of a room were not attached to either the apartment or the building.

From the door I could see the sharp line of the sun cutting off half the ceiling and a third of the floor with black shadow. Six months of permanent sun had warped the pine wardrobe and denuded the whitewashed walls to even greater whiteness.

And it was on one of the walls that, recoiling in surprise and revulsion, I saw the unexpected mural.

On the whitewashed wall by the door—that's why I hadn't seen them before—were charcoal outlines, in about life size, of a nude man, a nude woman, and a dog more nude than dogs really are. What the nudity disclosed was not drawn in on the bodies, the nudity came merely from the absence of all covering: they were the shapes of empty nudity. The lines were thick, made with a broken-tipped piece of charcoal. In places they were doubled, as though one line were the mark of the other's trembling. A dry trembling by dry charcoal.

The lines' rigidity fixed the outsized, crazy figures to the wall like three automatons. Even the dog had the tame insanity of something that is not powered by a force of its own. The clumsiness of the overbold lines made the dog seem to me something solid and petrified, set more in itself than on the wall.

After I got over the initial surprise of finding this hidden mural in my own home, I looked more closely, now with amused surprise, at these isolated figures on the wall. The simplified feet didn't quite touch the floor line, the small heads didn't reach the ceiling line, and that, along with the stupid rigidity of the lines, gave the three isolated figures the appearance of three mummies. As the figures' harsh motionlessness bothered me more and more, the notion of mummies grew stronger and stronger. They stood out as though they had gradually oozed forth from the inside of the wall, had slowly come from the core, finally reaching the harsh lime surface.

None of the figures was touching, and the three didn't form a group: each figure stared straight ahead, as though it had never looked sideways, as though it had never seen any of the others and had no idea that anyone existed beside it.

I gave a constrained smile, I was trying to smile: because each figure was there on the wall, just as I was there, standing rigid in the doorway. The drawing was not a decoration, it was writing.

I was assailed by a recollection of the absent maid. I tried to remember her face, and was amazed that I could not—she had been able to exclude me so completely from my own home that it was as if she had closed the door on me and left me far from my own lodging. Recollection of her features escaped me, it must be just a temporary lapse.

But her name . . . of course, of course I remembered, finally: it was Janair. And, looking at this hieratic drawing, I suddenly realized that Janair had hated me. I looked at the figures of the man and the woman, with the palms of their vibrant hands up and open, and they seemed to have been left there by Janair as a crude message for when I would open the door.

My discomfort was somehow amusing; had it never occurred to me that in Janair's silence there might have been a criticism of my life-style, which her silence must have labeled "a man's life"? how had she thought of me?

I looked at the drawing on the wall in which I was probably being portrayed . . . I, the Man. And the dog . . . was that the name she was calling me? For years I had been judged only by my peers and by my own circle, which were, in the final analysis, made by myself for myself. Janair was the first outside person whose gaze I really took notice of.

Suddenly, with, now, real discomfort, I finally allowed there to come over me a sensation that, through negligence and lack of interest, I had for a good six months not allowed myself to have: the sensation of that woman's silent hatred. What surprised me was that it was a kind of free hate, the worst kind of hate: indifferent hate. Not a hate that individualized me but just the absence of all compassion. No, not even hate.

That was when I unexpectedly succeeded in remembering her face, but, of course, how could I have forgotten it? I pictured again her quiet, black face, pictured her completely opaque skin that seemed more like one of her ways of being silent, extremely well defined eyebrows, I pictured again the fine, delicate features that were barely discernible on the faded blackness of her skin.

The features—I discovered with no pleasure—were a queen's features. And her posture as well: her body, erect, slim, hard, smooth, almost fleshless, with no breasts, or ass. And her clothes? It wasn't surprising that I had used her as though she had no presence: under her small apron she always wore dark brown or black, which made her all dark and invisible—I shivered to discover that till now I hadn't noticed that that woman was an invisible woman. Janair had what was almost only an external form, the features within that form were so refined that they barely existed: she was flattened out like a bas-relief frozen on a piece of wood.

And was it inevitable that just as she herself was, so she saw me? abstracting everything unessential from the body that was me drawn on the wall and also seeing only my outlines. Curiously, however, the figure on the wall still reminded me of someone: myself. Besieged by the presence of herself that Janair had left in a room in my home, I noticed that the three angular zombie figures had in fact kept me from going in, as though the room were still being occupied.

I hesitated at the door.

Also because the room's unexpected simplicity disoriented me: in fact I wouldn't even know where to start cleaning up, or even if it was necessary.

I looked about, dispirited, at the minaret's nakedness:

The bed, from which the bedding had been stripped, had its dusty cloth mattress exposed, with big, faded blotches like from sweat or watery blood, old, pale blotches. Here and there, strands of thick horsehair came through the cloth, which was so dry it was rotten, and they stood straight up in the air.

Along one of the walls, three old suitcases were stacked in so perfect a symmetrical order that I had just now perceived their presence, since they didn't change at all the sense of the room's emptiness. On them, and on the almost effaced mark of a "G. H.," a silent, sedimented accumulation of dust.

And then there was the narrow wardrobe: it had only one door and was as tall as a person of my height. The wood, continually dried out by the sun, had broken open in slits and cracks. Had that Janair never closed the window? She, even more than I, had taken advantage of the view from the "penthouse."

The room was so different from the rest of the apartment that going into it was like leaving my own home and entering another. The room was the opposite of what I had created in my home, the opposite of the gentle beauty that came from my talent for arrangement, from my talent for living, the opposite of my serene irony, my sweet, disinterested irony: it was a violation of my quotation marks, the quotation marks that made me a reference to myself. The room was the portrait of an empty stomach.

And nothing there had been done by me. In the rest of the apartment the sun filtered in from the outside in soft beam after soft beam, the result of the interaction of heavy curtains and light curtains. But here the sun didn't seem to come from outside to inside: this seemed to be the place where the sun itself was, fixed and unmoving, with a harsh light, as though the room didn't close its eyes, even at night. Everything here was dissected nerves that had had their ends dried into wire. I had been prepared to clean up a mess, but this struggle with its absence disoriented me.

I noticed at that point that I was irritated. The room bothered me physically, as though the sound of the scratching of dry charcoal on the dried whitewash still hung in the air. The room's inaudible sound was like the sound of a needle going around on a record after the music had finished playing. It was the neutral thing-screeching that made up the matter of its silence. Charcoal and fingernails together, charcoal and fingernails, calm, compact fury on the part of the woman who was the representative of a silence as if she represented a foreign country, the African queen. And she had taken up lodging here in my home, that stranger, that indifferent enemy.

I asked myself if Janair had in fact hated me — or if it had been I who had hated her, without even looking at her. Just as I was now discovering with irritation that the room didn't just irritate me, I detested it, that cubicle with nothing but surfaces: its innards had dried and shriveled up. I looked around me with repulsion and despair.

Until I forced myself to take heart . . . and a certain violence: all this would have to be changed this very day.

The first thing that I'd do would be to haul down the hallway the few things that were left in the room. Then I would throw bucket after bucket of water into the empty room and let the harsh air drink it up, and finally I would wet down the dust until some moisture came into that desert, destroying the minaret that so haughtily topped a horizon of roofs. Then I would throw water onto the wardrobe, swamp it in a flood up to mouth-level — and then, then watch the wood start to rot. An unexplainable anger, but one that had come over me completely naturally, had taken hold: I wanted to kill something here.

And then, then I would cover that dry-straw mattress with a soft, cold, clean sheet, one of my own sheets with my initials embroidered on it, to replace the one that Janair must have thrown into the wash.

But before all else I would scrape that granulated carbon dessication off the wall, scratching the dog off with a knife blade, erasing the man's hands with the turned-out palms, destroying the undersized head of that hideous naked woman. And I would throw water and more water until it ran in streams down the clean-scraped wall.

As though I were looking at a photograph of the room after I had changed it back into mine and into me, I gave a sigh of relief.

Then I went in.

How can I explain it except that something was happening that I don't understand. What did that woman who was me really want? what was happening to a G. H. in luggage leather?

Nothing, nothing, it was just that my nerves were now on edge — my nerves that had been calm, or just organized? had my silence really been a silence, or a loud voice that is mute?

How can I explain it to you? Suddenly that whole world that was me was contracting from exhaustion, I couldn't stand carrying it on my shoulders any longer . . . it, what? and I gave in to a tension that had always been there but I didn't know it. At that time there were beginning to take place in me — and still I didn't know it — the first signs of the collapse of subterranean limestone caves that were falling in under the weight of stratified archaeological layers — and the force of the first collapse lowered the corners of my mouth, made my arms fall. What was happening to me? I shall never be able to understand it, but there must be someone who can. And I shall have to create that someone who can inside myself.

In spite of having come into the room, I seemed to have come into a nothingness. Even inside it I somehow kept staying outside. As though it was not deep enough to hold me and left parts of me still in the hallway, in the greatest rejection I had ever experienced: I didn't fit.

At the same time, in looking at the low sky of the whitewashed ceiling, I felt I was suffocating with restriction and confinement. I needed my own home back. I forced myself to remember that I owned that room too, it was in my apartment: for I had walked to this room without leaving the apartment, without going up or down stairs. Unless there were some way of falling into a chasm horizontally, as if the building had twisted slightly and I had been tossed from door to door until I reached this highest one.

Stuck inside here by a web of spaces, I was forgetting the order that I had made up for getting things organized, and I didn't know for sure where to start. The room had no point that you could call its starting-place and none that you could call its end. It was of a sameness that made it undelimited.

I passed my gaze over the wardrobe, raised it to a crack in the ceiling, trying to get a better hold on that enormous, empty space. More boldly, but with no intimacy, I ran my fingers over the prickly mattress.

Then an idea came to me that gave me heart: the wardrobe, after it was well nourished with water, its fibers completely swollen out, I would wax it to give it some shine, and I'd even put a coat of wax on the inside, since it must be even more parched in there.

I opened the narrow wardrobe door a crack, and the dark inside came out like a breath of air. I tried to open it a little more, but the door was blocked because it hit against the foot of the bed. All of my head that would fit in I stuck through the crack that the door made. And, as though the darkness inside were spying on me, we remained for an instant spying on each other without seeing each other. I didn't see anything, I only noticed the hot, dry smell, like the smell of a live chicken. But I pushed the bed a little closer to the window and got the door open a few centimeters more.

Then, before I could even understand it, my heart turned white like hair turns white.

Then, before I could even understand it, my heart turned white like hair turns white.

Up against the face that I had thrust through the opening, right next to my eyes, in the semidarkness, the heavy cockroach moved. My scream was so muffled that it was only by the contrast with the silence that I realized I hadn't screamed. The scream had stayed pounding inside my chest.

Nothing, it was nothing—I immediately tried to calm myself in the face of my fear. It was just that I hadn't expected, in a house that had been meticulously disinfected against my dread of cockroaches, I hadn't expected this room to have been left out. No, it wasn't nothing. It was a cockroach slowly moving toward the crack.

By its enormity and slowness, it must have been a very old cockroach. In my primeval horror of cockroaches, I had learned to guess their ages and dangers, even at a distance; even though I had never really come face to face with a cockroach, I knew their life processes.

It was just that the sudden discovery of life within the nakedness of this room had frightened me as though I had discovered that the dead room was in fact fecund.

Everything else here had dried up—but one cockroach had remained. A cockroach so old it was immemorial. What had always disgusted me about cockroaches was that they were obsolete and at the same time still living. Knowing that they had been on Earth in the same form as they have today even before the first dinosaurs had appeared, knowing that the first man to come forth had found them crawling across the ground in hoards, knowing that they had seen the formation of the great deposits of coal and oil in the world, were there during the great glacial advances and retreats—peaceful resistance. I knew that cockroaches could go more than a month without food or water. And they could even survive on wood for food. And even after you step on them they come apart slowly and keep on walking all the while. Even when they freeze, after they thaw out they keep on going. For three hundred and fifty million years, they have reproduced with no change. When the world was practically naked, they walked slowly across it.

Just like here, in this naked, dessicated room, a virulent speck: on a clean test tube, a material speck.

I looked around the room, suspiciously. There was, then, this cockroach. Or cockroaches. Where? maybe behind the suitcases. One? two? how many? Behind the immovable silence of the suitcases, maybe a whole black pile of cockroaches. One motionless atop the one beneath. Layers of cockroaches—which suddenly reminded me of what I once discovered as a child when I lifted up the mattress I was sleeping on: the blackness of hundreds upon hundreds of bedbugs huddled one on top of another.

The recollection of my childhood poverty, with bedbugs, leaky roofs, cockroaches, and rats was like a prehistoric past of me, I had lived with the first creatures on earth.

One cockroach? more? but how many? I asked myself in a fury. I let my gaze move slowly over the naked room. No sound, no sign: but how many? No sound and still I clearly sensed an emphatic vibration that was the vibration of silence rubbing against silence. Hostility had taken me over. More than just not liking cockroaches: I really hate them. Besides, they are miniature versions of a huge animal. The hostility increased.

It wasn't I who rejected the room, as I had felt for an instant at the door. The room, with its secret cockroach, had repelled me. I had been repelled by the sight of a nakedness as strong as a mirage's nakedness; for it had not been the mirage of an oasis that I had seen but the mirage of a desert. Afterward, I had been immobilized by the harsh message on the wall: the figures with the hands spread out had been one of the series of sentinels at the door to the sarcophagus. I now understood that the cockroach and Janair were the room's true inhabitants.

No, I wouldn't do any cleaning—not if there were going to be cockroaches. The new maid could dedicate her first workday to this dusty, empty casket.

Even in the fierce heat of the sun, a wave of shivers ran through me: I hurried to leave that burning chamber.

It was my first physical act of fear, finally expressed, that revealed to me with surprise that I was afraid. And that plunged me into a greater fear—in trying to leave, between the wardrobe and the foot of the bed, I tripped and fell. The very possibility of a fall in this room of silence made my body recoil in profound dread—stumbling had turned my attempted flight into an act ill-fated in itself—could this be the way that "they," the inhabitants of the sarcophagus, had of keeping me from getting away? They were keeping me from getting out by using this one simple means: they left me completely free since they knew that I could no longer get out without stumbling and falling.

I wasn't really penned in, I was just cornered. As cornered as if they had fastened me here with the single, simple act of pointing a finger at me, at me and then at the spot.

I had experienced sensitivity to place before. When I was a child, I had suddenly had the sense that I was lying on a bed that was in a city that was on the Land that was in the World. Just as when I was a child, I now had the clear sense that I was completely alone in a house and that the house was high and free-floating in the air, and that this house had invisible cockroaches in it.

Before when I put myself in a place, I grew. This time I put myself in a place by shrinking—shrinking so much that the only space I took up in the room was between the foot of the bed and the wardrobe door.

But this time the sensitivity to place was, fortunately, not happening to me at night, as it had when I was a child, since it now had to be somewhere after ten in the morning.

And, unexpectedly, the coming hour of eleven took on a horror for me—just as with place, so too time became palpable, I wanted to flee like from inside of a clock, and I rushed awkwardly.

But to get out of the corner I had put myself in by opening the wardrobe door, I would have to close that door, which was pinning me against the bed leg: here I was, with no way clear, cornered by the sun, which was now burning the hair on the nape of my neck in an oven-blast called ten o'clock in the morning.

My quick hand moved to close the wardrobe door and open me a path—but it immediately drew back again.

For, inside the wardrobe, the cockroach moved.

I stayed quiet. My breathing was light, superficial. I now had the sense that my situation was hopeless. And I knew that, absurd though it might be, my only chance of getting out lay in facing up to the absurd fact that there was something irresolvable here. I knew that I had to recognize the danger I was in, even though I knew that it was crazy to believe in an entirely nonexistent danger. But I had to believe in myself—like everyone else, I had been in danger all my life—to get free this time, I had the mind-boggling responsibility of having to face that fact.

Closed in as I was between the wardrobe door and the foot of the bed, I hadn't yet given a second try at moving my feet to get out, but I had moved back, as though despite its extreme slowness the cockroach could swoop out in an instant—I had seen roaches that suddenly took off in flight: winged fauna.

I stayed there, still, plans racing madly through my mind. I was alert, I was completely alert. A great sense of hope arose inside me, and a surprised resignation: in this alert hope I recognized all my prior hope, I recognized too the attentiveness that I had experienced before, the attentiveness that never leaves me and that, in the final analysis, may be the thing that is most a part of my life—that perhaps is my very life itself. And then, the cockroach: what is the only sense a cockroach has? attentiveness to living, inseparable from its body. For me, anything that I had added to what was inseparable from me would probably never hold back that attentiveness which, more than an attentiveness to life, was my very life process itself.

It was then that the cockroach started to come out from inside.

It was then that the cockroach started to come out from inside.

First the annunciatory flutter of the antennae.

Then, behind those dry threads, the reluctant body started to appear. Until almost the whole thing was right at the opening of the wardrobe door.

It was grayish, it was hesitant, as though it carried enormous weight. It was now almost completely visible.

I quickly lowered my eyes. By hiding my eyes I hid from the cockroach the cunning stratagem that had just taken hold of me—my heart beat almost as with joy. For I had suddenly felt that I had some reserves, that I had never used them before—and now a latent power at last beat inside me and a greatness took me over: a greatness of courage, as if fear itself was what had finally provided me with courage. Just moments before, I had thought, superficially, that my only feelings were ones of indignation and disgust, but now I recognized—although I had never known it before—that what was happening was that I had finally taken on a huge fear, much greater than myself.

That huge fear completely pervaded me. Turned in upon myself, like a blind man listening to his own listening, I for the first time felt myself taken over by an instinct. And I shivered with great delight, as though I were finally in touch with the grandeur of an instinct that was horrible, totally and completely sweet—as though I were finally experiencing, and within myself, a grandeur greater than myself. I was for the first time becoming drunk with a hatred as clean as water from a spring, I was becoming drunk with the desire, justified or not, to kill.

An entire life of attentiveness—for fifteen centuries I hadn't fought, for fifteen centuries I hadn't killed, for fifteen centuries I hadn't died—an entire life of aloof attentiveness now came together inside me and rang, like a mute bell whose vibrations I didn't need to hear, for I recognized them. As though at last I was for the first time in balance with Nature.

A completely controlled rapaciousness had possessed me, and because it was controlled it was pure power. Up to then, I had never been mistress of my powers, powers that I neither understood nor wanted to understand, but the life in me had stored them up so that one day there would blossom forth this unknown, happy, unconscious matter that was, finally, me! me, whatever that might be.

Without any reticence at all, moved by my delivery over to what is wicked, without any reticence, moved, happy, I was for the first time being the unknown figure that I was . . . but, not knowing myself would no longer be an obstacle for me, the truth had just gone beyond the limits of myself: I raised my hand as though to take an oath, and in one move I slammed the door on the cockroach's half-protruding body . . .

Simultaneously, I had shut my eyes. And I stayed that way, all ashake. What had I done?

Could I have known right then that I wasn't referring to what I had done to the cockroach but instead to . . . what I had done to myself?

In those instants when my eyes were closed I became aware of myself like one becomes aware of a taste: I had through and through the taste of steel and malice, I was all acid, like a piece of metal sitting on your tongue, like a crushed green plant, my taste came full into my mouth. What had I done to myself? My heart pounding, my temples pulsing, I had done this to myself: I had killed. *I* had killed! But why this jubilation and, even more than it itself, why the vital acceptance of the jubilation? For how long, then, had I been primed to kill?

No, that wasn't the issue. The question was: what had I killed?

That calm woman that I had always been, had she gone crazy with pleasure? my eyes still closed, I was trembling with jubilation. Killing . . was so much greater than I, was of a piece with this measureless room. Killing had at last opened up the dry sands of this room to moisture, at last, as though I had dug and dug, with hard, avid fingers, until I found inside myself a potable stream of life that was the stream of a death. I slowly opened my eyes, now in sweetness, in gratitude, timidity, in a shyness of glory.

From the finally moist world from which I was emerging, I opened my eyes and encountered again the great, harsh, open light, I saw the wardrobe door, now closed.

And I saw the cockroach's front half sticking out of the door.

Sticking forward, erect in the air, a caryatid.

But a living caryatid.

At first I didn't understand, I just looked in surprise. Slowly I realized what had happened: I hadn't pushed the door hard enough. I had, to be sure, trapped the cockroach in the door so it couldn't come out any farther. But I had left it alive.

Alive and looking at me. I turned my eyes aside in a quick, violent reaction.

I still needed, then, the final stroke. One more thrust? I didn't look at the roach, but I kept telling myself that I needed one more thrust—I kept slowly telling myself that, as though every repetition worked to send a command order to my heartbeats, the beats that were spaced too much like a pain whose sensation I couldn't feel.

Until—succeeding at last in hearing myself, at last succeeding in giving myself orders—I lifted my arm up high, as if my entire body weight would come down on the wardrobe door along with the blow from my arm.

But it was then that I saw the cockroach's face.

It was aimed straight ahead, at the same level as my head and eyes. For an instant I paused with my hand poised in the air. Then, gradually, I lowered it.

An instant before I might not have been able to see the expression on the cockroach's face.

But it was too late by a split second: I had seen it. My hand, which came down when I stopped the blow, slowly rose again to my stomach: though I had not moved from the spot, my stomach had recoiled inside my body. My mouth had become too dry, I passed my tongue, which was also dry, over my rough lips.

It was a shapeless face. The antennae stuck out in whiskers at the sides of the mouth. The brown mouth was clearly demarcated. The thin, long whiskers moved about slow and dry. Its faceted black eyes looked around. It was a cockroach as old as a fossilized fish. It was a cockroach as old as salamanders, and chimeras, and griffins, and leviathans. It was as ancient as a legend. I looked at its mouth: there was the real mouth.

I had never seen a cockroach's mouth. I , in fact . . . I had never really seen a cockroach. I had only felt repugnance at their ancient, ever-present existence . . . but I had never come face to face with one, even in my mind.

And so I discovered that despite their compactness, they are made up of shell after shell, gray and thin, like the layers of an onion, as though you could lift one layer up with your fingernail and there would always be another one underneath, and another. Maybe those layers were the wings, but then it would be made up of layer after thin layer of wings compressed to form that compact body.

It was an auburn color. And all covered with cilia. Maybe the cilia were the multiple legs. The antennae were quiet now, dry, dusty filaments.

Cockroaches don't have noses. I looked at it, with that mouth of its, and its eyes: it looked like a dying mulatto woman. But its eyes were black and radiant. The eyes of a girl about to be married. Each eye itself looked like a cockroach. Each fringed, dark, live, dusted eye. And the other one just the same. Two cockroaches mounted on the cockroach, and each eye reproduced the entire animal.

Each eye reproduced the entire animal.

"Pardon my putting this all on you, hand that I have in mine, but I don't want to keep it for myself! take the cockroach, I want nothing to do with what I saw."

There I was, mouth agape, offended, drawn back— face-to-face with the dusty being that was looking back at me. Take away what I saw: for what I saw, with a compulsiveness so painful and so frightening and so innocent[what I saw was life looking back at me.]

How else could I refer to that horrible, brute raw matter and dry plasma that was simply there while I shrank back within myself in dry nausea, I sinking centuries and centuries deep in mud—it was mud, and not even dried mud but mud still wet, still alive, it was an ooze in which the roots of my identity were twisting about with intolerable slowness.

Take, take all that for yourself, I don't want to be a living person! I disgust myself, I marvel at myself, thick ooze coming slowly forth.

That's how it was, that's how it was, then. I had looked upon the live cockroach and had discovered in it my deepest life identity. In a difficult demolition, hard, narrow passages were opening inside me.

I looked at it, at the cockroach; I hated it so much that I was changing sides, forming solidarity with it, since I couldn't bear being alone with my own aggressiveness.

And all at once I groaned out loud, this time I heard my groan. My truest coherence was in fact rising up to the surface of me, like a pus—and I sensed, with fright and dread, that that "I-being" came from a source much prior to any human source, and, horribly, much greater than any human one as well.

There was opening out in me, with the slowness of stone gates, there was opening out in me the wide life of silence, the very life that was to be found in the stationary sun, the very one that was to be found in the motionless cockroach. And it could be the very same inside me! if I had the courage to abandon . . . to abandon my feelings? If I had the courage to abandon hope.

Hope in what? For the first time I had the great fear of feeling that I had based an entire hope on becoming something I was not. The hope—what other word is there for it?—that for the first time now I was going to abandon, through courage and through mortal curiosity. In my life up to now had that hope been grounded in a truth? With childish astonishment, I now . . . doubted.

To know what I really had to hope for, would I have to pass through my truth? To what extent had I up to now invented one destiny while in my depths living on another?

I closed my eyes, waiting for this strange feeling to pass, waiting for my panting to become something more than the panting in that groan that I had heard as though it were coming from the depths of a dry, deep cistern, just as the cockroach is the creature of a dry cistern. I kept feeling the groan, incalculably far within me, but it was no longer reaching my throat.

This is madness, I thought, with my eyes closed. But the sense of that birth from within the dust was so undeniable . . . that I could only follow what I knew very well was not madness but was, my God, a worse truth, the horrible truth. But why horrible? Because it wordlessly contradicted everything I had been accustomed, also wordlessly, to think.

I waited for the strange feeling to pass, for health to return. But I recognized, with a long-forgotten force of memory, that I had felt this feeling before: it was the same feeling I had had when I saw my own blood outside myself, and I was shocked by it. For the blood that I saw outside myself, that blood I wondered at with such attraction: it was my own.

I didn't want to open my eyes again, I didn't want to keep on seeing. The rules and laws, it was important not to forget them, you have to remember that without the rules and laws there would also be no order, it was important for me not to forget them and, in order to defend myself, to defend them.

But the fact was that I could no longer hold myself down.

The first tie had already involuntarily broken, and I was loosening myself from law, even though I suspected that I would be going into the inferno of living matter—what sort of inferno awaited me? but I had to go. I had to fall into my soul's condemnation, curiosity was consuming me.

Then, all at once, I opened my eyes and saw full-on the room's limitless vastness, that room that resounded in silence—Hellish laboratory.

The room, the unexpected room. My entrance into it had finally become complete.

This room had only one way in, and it was a narrow one: through the cockroach. The cockroach that filled the room with a resonance that was in the last analysis open, the resonances of its rattlesnake bells in the desert. By a perilous road I had reached the deep breach in the wall that was that room . . . and the break formed a wide natural hall like in a cave.

Bare, as though prepared for only one person's entrance. And whoever came in would be transformed into a "she" or into a "he." I was the person the room called "she." I had come in an "I," but the room then gave me the dimensions of "she." As though I were also the other side of a cube, the side that you don't see because you are seeing the front side.

And, in my great expansion, I was on the desert. How can I make you understand? I was on the desert as I had never been before. It was a desert that called me like a monotonous, remote canticle calls. I was being seduced. And I went toward that enticing madness. But my fear was not the fear of someone who was going toward madness and thus toward a truth—my fear was the fear of having a truth that I would come to despise, a defamatory truth that would make me get down and exist at the level of the cockroach. My first contact with truths always defamed me.

"Hold my hand tight, because I feel that I'm going. I am again going to the most primary divine life, I am going to an inferno of brute life. Don't let me see because I am close to seeing the core of life—and through the cockroach, which I am now beginning to see again, through that sample of calm, live fear, I am afraid that in that core I won't know anymore what hope is."

The cockroach is pure seduction. Cilia, blinking cilia that beckon.

I too, gradually reducing myself to what was irreducible in me, I too had thousands of cilia blinking, and with my cilia I advance, I protozoic, pure protein. Hold my hand tight, I have reached the irreducible with the fatefulness of a deathknell—I sense that all this is ancient and immense, I sense in the hieroglyph of the slow cockroach the writing of the Far East. And in this desert of great seductions, the creatures: I and the live cockroach. Life, my love, is one great seduction where everything that exists is seduced. That room that was desert and therefore primitively alive. I had reached nothingness, and the nothingness was live and moist.

I had reached nothingness, and the nothingness was live and moist.

It was then — it was then that the pulp started slowly to come out of the cockroach I had smashed, like out of a tube.

The cockroach's pulp, which was its insides, raw matter that was whitish and thick and slow, was piling up on it as though it were toothpaste coming out of the tube.

Before my nauseated, attracted eyes, the cockroach's form, as it grew on the outside, kept slowly changing. The white matter was slowly spreading across its back, like a load set for it to carry. Pinched in place, it was increasingly carrying on its dusty back a load that was in fact its own body.

"Scream," I silently commanded myself. "Scream," I told myself again with a sigh of deep quietude.

The white mass had stopped piling up on top of the shell. I looked up to the ceiling, resting for a while eyes that I could feel had grown great and deep.

But if I had screamed, even if only once, I might never have been able to stop. If I had screamed, nobody could have done anything to help me; as it is, if I never reveal my lacking, no one will become frightened of me, and they'll help me without knowing it; but only so long as I don't frighten anyone by going beyond the rules. But if they know, they become frightened, we who keep our screams inviolable secrets. If I give the call of alarm of someone living, they will drag me along silently and harshly, for that is what they do to anyone who crosses the lines of the permissible world, the exceptional being is dragged along, the being who screams.

I looked up to the ceiling with heavy eyes. Everything was summed up fiercely in my never uttering an initial scream—a first scream sets off all the others, the first scream of birth sets off a life, if I were to scream it would awaken thousands of screaming beings who would unleash a chorus of screams and horror all along the rooftops. If I screamed, it would unleash existence—the existence of what? the existence of the world. For myself, I reverently feared the existence of the world.

"The fact, oh hand that gives me strength, the fact is that, in an experience that I would like to forget, an experience for which I ask forgiveness of myself, I was leaving *my* world and going into *the* world."

The fact is that I was no longer seeing myself, I was just seeing. An entire civilization that had been set up having as its guarantee that one should immediately mix what one sees with what one feels, an entire civilization that has self-salvation as its foundation stone—I was now in its debris. The only person who can get out of that civilization is one whose special function is getting out: a scientist is given the chance, a priest has permission. But not a woman who hasn't the guarantee that such titles bring. And I fled, regretfully, I fled.

If you knew the loneliness of those first steps I took. It wasn't like a person's loneliness. It was as though I had died and was taking my first steps alone into another life. And it was as though they called that loneliness glory, and I too knew that it was a kind of glory, and I shook all over with that primary, divine glory that I not only did not understand but also profoundly wanted to reject.

"Because, look, I knew that I was entering the crude, raw glory of nature. Seduced, I nonetheless struggled as much as I could against the shifting sands that were sucking me down: and every move that I made toward 'no, no,' every new move pushed me inexorably; not having the strength to struggle was my only pardon."

I looked around the room in which I had been imprisoned and looked for a way out, desperately looked to escape, and within myself I had already retreated so far that my soul had flattened itself against the wall . . . without even being able to stop myself, without even wanting to stop anymore, fascinated by the control of the magnet that was pulling me, I retreated within myself, up against the wall, onto which I grafted myself in the design of the woman. I had retreated all the way to the marrow of my bones, my last redoubt. Where, on the wall, I was so naked that I cast no shadow.

And the dimensions, the dimensions remained the same, I could feel that they were, I knew that I had never been anything other than that woman on the wall, I was her. And I was completely perpetuated, a long, fecund road.

My tension suddenly broke, like a noise cut off.

And the first real silence began to blow. That tranquil, vast, strange something that I had seen in my dim, smiling, photographs — that something was outside of me for the first time and entirely within my reach, incomprehensible but within my reach.

What assuaged me, like slaking a thirst, assuaged me as though all my life I had been waiting for a water as vital for the bristling body as cocaine is for someone crying out for it. At last, the body, imbued with silence, found peace. Relief came from my fitting into the silent design of that cavern.

Up to that moment I had not fully seen my struggle, so immersed had I been in it. But now, because of the silence into which I had finally fallen, I knew that I had been struggling, that I had succumbed, and that I had given in.

And that, as of right now, I was really in the room.

As much a part of it as a drawing made three million years ago in a cave. And that is how I fit within myself, and how within my very self I was etched on that wall.

The narrow passage had been the daunting cockroach, and I had slipped with disgust through that body of scales and ooze. And I had ended up, all impure myself, embarking, through it, upon my past, which was my continuous present and my continuous future—and which, today and ever, is on the wall, and my fifteen million daughters, from that time down to myself, were also there. My life had been as continuous as death. Life is so continuous that we divide it into stages and call one of them death. I had always been in life, it mattered little that it was not I properly speaking, not that thing that I customarily call "I." I had always been in life.

I, neutral cockroach body, I with a life that at last is not eluding me because I finally see it outside myself—I am the cockroach, I am my leg, I am my hair, I am the section of brightest light on the wall plaster—I am every Hellish piece of myself—life is so pervasive in me that if they divide me in pieces like a lizard, the pieces will keep on shaking and writhing. I am the silence etched on a wall, and the most ancient butterfly flutters in and looks at me: just the same as always. From birth to death is what I call human in myself, and I shall never actually die.

But this is not eternity, it is condemnation.

How opulent this silence is. It is the accumulation of centuries. It is the silence of a cockroach looking. The world looks at itself in me. Everything looks at everything, everything experiences the other; in this desert things know things. Things know things as much as this . . . this something that I shall call pardon, if I wish to save myself within the human plan. It is pardon in itself. Pardon is one of the attributes of living matter.

Pardon is one of the attributes of living matter.

"See here, my precious, see how I am organizing for fear, see how I still cannot touch those primary laboratory elements without immediately trying to put a hope together. So as of yet my inner metamorphosis makes no sense. In such a metamorphosis, I lose everything I have had, and what I have had has been myself—all that I have ☆ is what I am. And what am I now? I am: a standing in the presence of fear. I am: what I have seen. I don't understand and I am afraid to understand, the matter of the world frightens me, with its planets and its cockroaches."

I, who before lived on words of charity, or pride—or something. But what an abyss between the word and what it sought to do, what an abyss between the word love and the love that does not even have a human sense—because—because love is living matter. Is love living matter?

What was it that happened to me yesterday? and now? I'm confused, I have crossed desert after desert, but have I remained trapped under some detail? like under a rock.

No, wait, wait: I must remember with relief that

since yesterday I have left that room, I have got out, I'm free! and I still have a chance to get it all back. If I want to.

But do I want to?

What I have seen is unorganizable. But if I really want to, right now, I can still translate it into terms that would be more like ours, into human terms, and I can still put aside those hours of yesterday. If I still want to, I can ask myself in another way, a way that is within our language, what happened to me.

And, if I question myself that way, I can still have an answer that will get it all back. That recovery would be to acknowledge that G. H. was a woman who lived well, well, well, who lived in the top layer of the world's sands, and the sands had never given way beneath her feet; the harmony was such that when the sands moved her feet moved in concert with them, so everything stayed firm and compacted. G. H. lived on the top floor of a superstructure, and, even though it was built in the air, it was a solid building, she herself too in the air, like bees weave their life in the air. And the same thing had been happening for centuries, with the necessary or incidental variations, and it worked. It worked—at least nothing spoke, and no one spoke, no one said "no": so, it worked.

But precisely the slow accumulation of centuries automatically piling up was what was making that building in the air very heavy, without anyone noticing, that building was becoming saturated with itself: it was becoming more and more compacted instead of more and more fragile. The accumulation of living in a superstructure was becoming ever closer to too heavy to stay in the air.

Like a building with all its occupants sleeping securely at night not knowing that its foundations are sagging and, at one instant unannounced by their tranquility, the beams will give way because the building's cohesion is slowly being pulled apart, a millimeter per century. And then, when it's least expected—in an instant as repetitiously habitual as the instant of raising a drinking glass to your smiling lips while at a dance—then, yesterday, a day as sun-filled as these days at the height of summer usually are, with men working and kitchens giving off smoke and the jackhammer breaking the stones and the children laughing and a priest trying to prevent, but to prevent what?—yesterday, without warning, there was the crash of solidness suddenly become crumbly in demolition.

In the collapse, tons fell upon tons. When I, G. H. even on my luggage, I, one of the people, opened my eyes, I was—not on top of the rubble, for even the rubble had been swallowed up by the sands—I was on a quiet plain, kilometers and kilometers below what had been a great city. Things had gone back to being what they had been.

The world had reclaimed its own reality, and, just like after a catastrophe, my culture had ended: I was merely a historical fact. Everything in me had been reclaimed by the beginning of time and by my own beginning. I had passed on to a first, primary plane, I was in the silence of the winds and in the age of tin and copper—at the first age of life.

Listen, in the presence of the living cockroach, the worst discovery was that the world is not human, and that we are not human.

No, don't be afraid! What had saved me up to that moment in the sentimentalized life that I had lived on was doubtless that the inhuman is our better part, is the thing, the thing part of people. It was only because of that that I, like a false person, had not by then sunk under my sentimentalistic and utilitarian constitution: my human sentiments were utilitarian, but I had not foundered because the thing part, God-matter, was too strong and was waiting to reclaim me. The great neutral punishment of life in general is that it can suddenly undermine a specific life; if it is not given strength of its own, then it bursts like a dike bursts—and becomes pure, with no admixture: purely neutral. That was the great danger: when that neutral thing part does not filter through a personal life, all that life can become pure neutrality.

But exactly why had the first silence come suddenly to be remade in me? As if one quiet woman had simply been called and had quietly stood up, left her embroidery on her chair, and, without a word—leaving her life, abandoning embroidery, love, and priorly constituted soul—without a word that woman had calmly got down on all fours and begun to go about that way, and to crawl with calm, glaring eyes: that prior life had reclaimed her and she had gone.

But why me? But why *not* me. If it hadn't been me, I wouldn't have known, and since it was me, I found out— that's all there is to it, nothing more. What was it that had called me: madness or reality?

Life was taking its vengeance on me, and that vengeance consisted merely in coming back, nothing more. Every case of madness involves something coming back. People who are possessed are not possessed by something that just comes but instead by something that comes back. Sometimes life comes back. If in me everything crumbled before that power, it is not because that power was in itself necessarily an overwhelming one: it in fact had only to come, since it had already become too full-flowing a force to be controlled or contained—when it appeared it overran everything. And then, like after a flood, there floated a wardrobe, a person, a loose window, three suitcases. And that seemed like Hell to me, that destruction of layers and layers of human archaeology.

Hell, because the world held no more human sense for me, and man held no more human sense for me. And in the absence of that humanization and in the absence of that sentimentalization of the world—I become terrified.

Without a scream, I looked at the cockroach.

Looked at up close, the cockroach is an object of great opulence. A bride with black jewelry. It is completely unique, it seems one of a kind. By pinching the middle of its body in the wardrobe door, I had isolated the only specimen. All that showed was half its body. The rest that was not in view could have been huge and been in thousands of homes, behind things and wardrobes. I, however, did not want the part that had come to be mine. Behind the surfaces of buildings—those dusky jewels scraping along the ground?

I felt impure, as the Bible speaks of the impure. Why did the Bible spend so much time on the impure, even to making a list of impure and forbidden animals? Why, if, like all the rest, they too had been created? And why was the impure forbidden? I had committed the forbidden act of touching something impure.

I had committed the forbidden act of touching something impure.

And so impure was I, in my sudden, indirect moment of self-knowledge, that I opened my mouth to call for help. They proclaim; the Bible does, they proclaim, but if I understand what they proclaim, it will be they who call me crazy. People like me had proclaimed, but understanding them would be my destruction.

"But you shall not eat of the impure: which are the eagle, the griffin, and the hawk." Nor the owl, nor the swan, nor the bat, nor the stork, nor the entire tribe of crows.

I knew that the Bible's impure animals were forbidden because the impure is the root—for there are things created that have never made themselves beautiful and have stayed just as they were when created, and only they still continue to be the entirely complete root. And because they are the entirely complete root, they are not to be eaten, the fruit of good and of evil—eating of living matter would expel me from a paradise of adornments and lead me to walk forever through the desert with a shepherd's staff. Many have been those who have walked in the desert with a staff.

Or even worse—it would lead me to see that the desert too is alive and has moisture, and to see that everything is alive and is made of the same thing.

To build a possible soul—a soul whose head will not devour its own tail—the law commands that one use only what is patently alive. And the law commands that whoever partakes of the impure must do so without knowing. For he who partakes of the impure knowing that it is impure . . . must also come to know that the impure is not impure. Is that it?

"And everything that crawls on the ground and has wings shall be impure and shall not be eaten."

I opened my mouth in fright: to ask for help. Why? because I did not want to become impure like the cockroach? what ideal held me to the sensing of an idea? why should I not make myself impure, exactly as I was revealing my whole self? What was I afraid of? being impure with what?

✳ impurity

Being impure with joy.

For now I understand that what I had begun to feel was joy, which I still had not yet recognized or understood. In my silent call for help, what I was struggling against was a vague first joy that I did not want to sense in myself because, albeit vague, it was already horrible: it was a joy without redemption, I don't know how to make it clear for you, but it was a joy without hope.

"Oh, don't pull your hand away from me, I've promised myself that maybe by the end of this impossible narrative I shall understand, oh maybe it will be on Hell's road that I shall be able to find what we need—but don't pull your hand away, even though I now know that the finding has to come on the road of what we are, if I can succeed in not sinking completely into what we are."

See, my love, I am losing the courage to find whatever it is I shall have to find, I am losing the courage to give myself over to the road itself, and I am now promising us that in that Hell I shall find hope.

"Perhaps it is not the ancient hope. Perhaps it cannot even be called hope."

I was struggling because I did not want an unknown joy. It would be as forbidden by my future salvation as the forbidden beast that was called impure—and I was opening and closing my mouth in torture to call for help, but then it still hadn't occurred to me to invent this hand that I have now invented to hold mine. In my fear yesterday I was alone, and I wanted to ask for help against my first dehumanization.

Dehumanization is as painful as losing everything, as losing everything, my love. I was opening and closing my mouth to call for help but I neither could nor knew how to enunciate.

The problem was that I no longer had anything to say. My agony was like the agony of trying to talk before dying. I knew that I was leaving something forever, something was going to die, and I wanted to pronounce the word that would at least capture that thing that was dying.

Finally I at least succeeded in articulating a thought: "I am asking for help."

Then it occurred to me that I had nothing to ask for help against. I had nothing to ask.

Suddenly, this was it. I was understanding that "ask" was a leftover from an entreatable world, which was becoming more and more remote. And if I continued trying to ask, it was to cling to the remainders of my old culture, to cling so tight that I wouldn't be pulled along by what was now reclaiming me. And to which—in a pleasure without hope—I was now giving in, oh I now wanted to give in—to have experienced it was now the beginning of a Hell of wanting, wanting, wanting . . . Was my will to want stronger than my will to salvation?

Every time I tried, I had nothing to ask for. And I saw, in fascination and horror, the pieces of my rotten mummy clothes fall dry to the floor; I witnessed my own metamorphosis from chrysalis to moist larva, my wings slowly drying and opening out. And a completely new belly made for the ground, a new belly was being reborn.

Without turning my eyes away from the cockroach, I lowered myself until I felt my body meet the bed and, without turning my eyes away from the cockroach, I sat down.

Now it was with eyes raised that I looked at it. Now, bent over on top of its own middle, it looked me end to end. I had trapped in front of myself the impure of the world — and I had disenchanted the living thing. I had lost my ideas.

Then, again, another full millimeter of white matter spurted out.

Then, again, another full millimeter of white matter spurted out.

Holy Mary, mother of God, I offer you my life in exchange for that moment yesterday's being untrue. The cockroach covered with the white matter was looking at me. I don't know if it saw me, I don't know what a cockroach sees. But the two of us were looking at each other, and I also don't know what a woman sees. But if its eyes didn't see me, its existence existed me: in the primary world that I had entered, beings exist other beings as a way of seeing one another. And in that world that I was coming to know, there are various modes that mean *to see*: one being looking at the other without seeing it, one possessing the other, one eating the other, one simply being in a corner and the other being there too: all that also means to see. The cockroach didn't see me directly, it was with me. The cockroach saw me not with its eyes but with its body.

And I . . . I saw. There was no way not to see it. There was no way to deny it: my convictions and my wings were drying out quickly: that was all they were there for. There was no way to deny it any longer. I don't know what it was that I could no longer deny, but I could no longer.

Nor could I any longer save myself, like before, with a whole culture that would help me to deny what I was seeing.

I was seeing all of it, the cockroach.

A cockroach is an ugly, shiny being. The cockroach is inside out. No, no, I don't mean that it has an inside and an outside; I mean that is what it is. What it had on the outside is what I hide inside myself: I have made my outside into a hidden inside. It was looking at me. And it wasn't a face. It was a mask. A deep sea diver's mask. That precious, rusty-colored gem. The two eyes were alive like two ovaries. It looked at me with the blind fertility of its look. It was making my dead fertility fertile. Could its eyes be salty? If I touched them—since I was slowly becoming more and more impure anyway—if I touched them with my mouth, would I taste salt in them?

I had tasted a man's eyes with my mouth and could tell that he was crying by the saltiness.

But, as I thought about the salt in the cockroach's black eyes, I suddenly recoiled again, and my dry lips curled back all the way to my teeth: the reptiles that move across the earth! In the stationary reverberation of light in the room, the cockroach was a small, slow crocodile. The dry, resonating room. I and the cockroach poised in that dryness, like on the dry crust of an extinct volcano. That desert I had gone into, and there I had also discovered life and its salt.

Again the white part of the cockroach squirted out, probably less than a millimeter.

This time, I barely, barely noticed the tiny outward movement that the matter made. I looked on, absorbed, silent.

"Never, before that time, had life happened to me during the daytime. Never in sunlight. Only, at night had the world slowly turned for me. Only, what would happen in the blackness of night itself also simultaneously happened in my own innards, and my blackness became undifferentiated from the outside blackness, and, in the morning when I opened my eyes, the world kept right on being a surface: the secret night life soon receded in my mouth to being the taste of a disappearing nightmare. But now life was happening in the daytime. Undeniable, there to see. Unless I turned my eyes away."

And I could still turn my eyes away.

"But Hell already had hold of me, my sweet, the Hell of a morbid curiosity. I was already disposing of my human soul, because seeing had begun to consume me with pleasure, I was selling my future, selling my salvation, selling us."

"I am calling for help," I suddenly shouted to myself, with the silence of those who have their mouths slowly drifted full of shifting sand, "I am calling for help," I thought, quiet and calm. But never once did it occur to me that I might get up and leave, as though that would be impossible. The cockroach and I had been buried in a mine cave-in."

The scale suddenly had only one plate. On that side was my deep rejection of cockroaches. But "rejection of cockroaches" was merely a set of words, and I also knew that at the time when I myself died I too would be untranslatable into words.

Of my own death, yes, I was indeed aware, for death was the future and is imaginable, and I had always had time to imagine. But the instant, the very instant—the right now—*that* is unimaginable, between the right now and the I there is no space: it is just now, inside me.

"Understand me, I had death down pat and death was no longer demanding of me. But what I had never experienced before was this running up against the moment called 'right now.' Today places demands on me today. I had never before realized that the moment of living too has no words. The moment of living, my love, was becoming so 'now' that I was putting my mouth into the matter of life. The moment of living is a ceaseless, slow creaking of doors continually opening wide open. Two gates were opening and had never stopped opening. But they continually opened out on . . . on nothingness?"

The moment of living is so Hellishly inexpressive that it is nothingness. What I called "nothingness," however, was so plastered to me that was it . . . me, to me? and therefore became invisible, like I was invisible to myself, and became nothingness. The doors kept on opening, as always.

Finally, my love, I fell. And it became a "now."

Finally, my love, I fell. And it became a now.

It was finally now. It was simply now. It was like this: the country was at 11:00 A.M. Superficially like a green yard, of the most delicate superficiality. Green, green—green is a yard. Between myself and that green, the water of the air. The green water of the air. I see everything through a full glass. And nothing is to be heard. In the rest of the house, shadows are all swollen. Ripe superficiality. It is 11:00 A.M. in Brazil. It is now. That means exactly now. Now is time swollen as far as it can be swollen. 11:00 has no depth. 11:00 is full of eleven hours up to the brim of the green glass. Time quivers like a stationary balloon. The air, fertile and panting. Until, with a national anthem, the tolling of 11:30 cuts the balloon's restraining ropes. And suddenly we'll all reach noon. Which will be green like now.

I suddenly awoke from the unexpected green oasis where I had for a moment completely hidden myself.

But I was on the desert. And now is not only at the heart of an oasis; now is also on the desert, and fully. It was right now. For the first time in my life there was a full now. This was the greatest brutality that I had ever come up against.

For nowness brings no hope, and nowness brings no future: the future will be precisely a now again.

I was so frightened that I became even quieter inside. For it seemed to me that I was finally going to have to feel.

It seems that I shall have to give up everything I leave on the other side of the gates. And I know, I knew, that if I went through the always-open gates, I would go into the heart of nature.

I knew that going in is no sin. But it is perilous, like dying. Just as we die without knowing where we go, and that is a body's greatest courage. To go in was a sin only because it was the condemnation of my life, and I might never after be able to return to it. Perhaps I already knew that, from those gates onward, there would be no difference between me and the cockroach. Either in my eyes or in the eyes of him who is God.

That was how I was taking my first steps into nothingness. My first hesitant steps in the direction of Life, and abandoning my own life. My foot stepped out into the air, and I went into paradise, or Hell: into the heart.

I ran my hand over my forehead: I noticed with relief that I had finally started to sweat. Up to a little bit earlier there had been only that hot dryness that dessicated us both. Now I started to become wet.

Oh, how exhausted I am! What I would really like now would be to cut all this off and put into this most difficult of stories, for pure diversion and relaxation, a positive tale that I heard one day—one of those tales about why some couple separated. Oh, I know so many interesting tales. And too, for a break, I could talk about tragedy. I know tragedies.

My sweat gave me relief. I looked up, to the ceiling. The ceiling had rounded out with the play of shafts of light and changed into something that reminded me of a vaulted ceiling. The heat's vibration was like the resonance of an oratorio being sung. Only my hearing apparatus sensed. A canticle with closed mouth, sound deafly resonating like something held fast and contained, amen, amen. A canticle of thanksgiving for the murder of one being by another being.

The most profound of murders: one that is a mode of relating, a way of one being existing the other being, a way of our seeing each other and being each other and having each other, a murder where there is neither victim nor executioner but instead a link of mutual ferocity. My primary struggle for life. "Lost in the Fiery Hell of a Canyon a Woman Struggles Desperately for Life."

I waited for that silent, trapped sound to go away. But the vastness grew within the small room, the mute oratorio opened it out in vibrations that reached the crack in the ceiling. The oratorio wasn't a prayer: it didn't ask for anything. Passions in the form of an oratorio.

The cockroach suddenly vomited another white, soft spurt through its crack.

"Oh, but whom could I go to for help, if you too," I then thought, in the direction of a man who once was mine, "if you too won't be able to help me now. For, like me, you tried to transcend life, and thus you got beyond it. But I'm not going to be able to do that anymore, I'm going to have to know, and I'll have to go on without you, even though I have tried to ask you for help. Pray for me, my mother, for not transcending is a sacrifice, and transcendence used to be my human effort at salvation, there was an immediate utility in transcendence. Transcendence is a transgression. But staying within what there is, that forces me not to be afraid!"

And I am going to have to stay within what there is.

Something must be said, don't you feel that something must be understood? oh, even if later on I have to go beyond it, even if later I transcend it, let it be fatefully born from me like the breath of a living person.

But, after what I know, shall I consider it the exhalation of breathing, or a miasma? no, not a miasma, I have pity on myself! I want, if transcendence comes fatefully upon me, for it to be like the breath born from my own mouth, the mouth that exists, and not from a false mouth opened up in an arm or in a head.

It was with Hellish joy that I was almost on the verge of dying. I started to feel that my ghostly step would be irreversible, and that I was leaving my human salvation behind little by little. I felt that my inside, despite being soft, white matter, nonetheless had the strength to burst my face of silver and of beauty, good-bye worldly beauty! Beauty that is now far from me and that I no longer want—I am unable to want beauty anymore—maybe I really never wanted it, but it was so nice! I recall how the game of beauty was nice, beauty was a continual transmutation.

But I give it up with Hellish relief. What has come out of the cockroach's belly is not something that can be transcended—oh, I don't mean that it is the opposite of beauty, "opposite to beauty" doesn't even make sense— what has come out of the cockroach is: "today," blessed be the fruit of your womb—I want nowness without decorating it with a future that will redeem it or with a hope—up to now what hope wanted in me was merely to sidestep nowness.

But I want much more than that: I want to find redemption in today, in right now, in the reality that is happening, and not in promise, I want to find joy in this instant—I want God in that stuff that is coming out of the cockroach's belly—even if, in my aged, human terms, that means the worst and, in human terms, Hell.

Yes, I wanted that. But at the same time,I held the stomach's mouth with my two hands: "I can't!" I implored another man who also never could and never would himself. "I can't! I don't want to know what that something that up to now I would call nothingness is made of!" I don't want to feel directly in my so delicate mouth the salt of the cockroach's eyes, because, Mother mine, I had accustomed myself to the saturation of the layers and not to the thing's simple moistness.

It was thinking about the salt in the cockroach's eyes, which, with the sigh of one who is going to be forced to give in yet again, I realized was still using the old human beauty: salt.

I would have to abandon the beauty of salt and the beauty of tears as well. That too, for what I was seeing was back before the human.

For what I was seeing was back before the human.

No, there was no salt in those eyes. I was absolutely sure that the cockroach's eyes were completely without taste. I had always cultivated salt, salt was the transcendence that I used to sense a taste and to run from what I called "nothingness." I cultivated salt, I had construed myself around salt. But what my mouth couldn't take in . . . was insipidity. What I was completely unprepared for . . . was the neutral.

And that neutral was the life I had been calling "nothingness." The neutral was Hell.

The sun had moved a bit and fixed itself on my back. The halved cockroach was also in the sun. I can't do anything for you, roach. I don't want to do anything for you.

But it was no longer a matter of doing anything: the cockroach's neutral look told me that that wasn't the question, and I knew it. It was just that I couldn't tolerate just staying seated there, just being, and so I wanted to do something. Doing something would be transcending, transcending is a way out.

But the moment had arrived for that not to be the question any longer. For the cockroach knew nothing of hope or of pity. If it wasn't pinned there and was bigger than I was, it would kill me with a busy, neutral pleasure. Just like the violent neutrality of its life allowed me, because I wasn't trapped and was bigger, to kill it. That was the kind of tranquil, neutral ferocity there was on the desert where we were.

And its eyes were insipid, not salty as I would have preferred: salt would be sentiment, and word, and taste. I knew that the cockroach's neutrality has the same tastelessness as its white matter. Sitting there, I was being formed. Sitting there, being formed, I knew that when I didn't call things salty or sweet, sad or happy or painful, or use even subtler shadings—only then would I not be transcending anymore and would I be staying within the thing itself.

That thing whose name I know not was what, as I sat there looking at the cockroach, I was now becoming able to call without a name. Contact with that thing with no qualities and no attributes was repugnant to me, the living thing without name or taste or smell was disgusting. Insipidity: taste was no longer anything more than an aftertaste: my own aftertaste. For one instant, then, I felt a kind of shocked happiness throughout my body, a horrible, happy indisposition in which my legs seemed to disappear, just as always happened when the roots of my unknown identity were touched.

Oh, at least I had now come to the point in the nature of the cockroach where I no longer wanted to do anything for it. I was freeing myself from my morality, and that was a catastrophe without uproar and without tragedy.

Morality. Wouldn't it be simpleminded to think that the moral problem in relation to others consists of acting as you ought to act and that the moral problem in relation to yourself is to try to feel as you ought to feel? Am I moral to the extent that I do what I should and feel what I should?

Suddenly, the moral question seemed to me not so much overwhelming as extremely insignificant. The moral problem, if we are to relate to it, ought to be both less demanding and greater. For as an ideal it is at one and the same time insignificant and unattainable. Insignificant should it be reached; unattainable because it cannot be reached. "Scandal still is necessary, but woe unto him through whom the scandal cometh"—was it the Old Testament that said that? The solution had to be a secret one. The ethics of morality are to keep it a secret. Freedom is a secret.

Although I know that, even in secret, freedom does not absolve guilt. But one must be greater than guilt. My least divine part is greater than my human guilt. God is greater than my essential guilt. I therefore prefer God to my guilt. Not to excuse myself and get away but because guilt lessens me.

I now wanted to do nothing for the cockroach. I was freeing myself from my morality—even though that caused fear, curiosity, and fascination in me, and a great deal of fear. I'm not going to do anything for you, I too scrape along the ground. I'm not going to do anything for you because I no longer know the meaning of love like I thought I did before. And too, what I thought I knew about love, that too I am leaving behind, I almost no longer know what it is, I no longer remember.

Maybe I'll find another name, so much crueler right from the outset, so much more the thing itself. Or maybe I won't find one. Is love when you don't give a name to things' identity?

But I now know something horrible: I know what it's like to need, need, need. And it's a new need, on a level that I can only call neutral and terrible. It's a need with no pity for my needing and no pity for the cockroach's needing. I was sitting there, quiet, sweating, precisely like now—and I see that there is something more serious, more fateful, and more central than everything that I have been in the habit of calling by names. I who called my hopes for love "love."

But now, it is within this neutral nowness of nature, and of the cockroach, and of my body's living sleep, that I want to know love. And I want to know if hope was a temporization with the impossible. Or if it was a putting-off of what is possible right now—and I haven't reached only for fear. I want a present moment that is not something with a promise but that *is*, that *is being*. That is the heart of what I want and I fear. That is the heart that I never sought.

The cockroach was touching me through with its black, faceted, shiny, neutral look.

And now I began to let it touch me. In fact, I had struggled all my life against the deep desire to let myself be touched—and I had struggled because I wasn't able to allow the death of what I called my goodness; the death of human goodness. But now I didn't want to fight against it anymore. There had to be a goodness so other that it wouldn't resemble goodness. I didn't want to fight anymore.

With disgust, with despair, with courage, I gave in. I had waited too long, and now I wanted to.

Did I want to only at that very moment? No, or else I would have left the room long ago, or simply would have scarcely noticed the cockroach—how many times before had I come across cockroaches and turned in another direction? I gave in, but with a fear and a sundering.

I thought that if the telephone should ring, I would have to answer it and could still be saved! But, like recalling a bygone world, I remembered that I had taken the receiver off the hook. If it hadn't been for that, it might ring,

I could run out of the room to answer it, and never, oh never again would I come back in.

"I remember you, when I kissed your man-face, slowly, slowly kissed it, and when the moment came to kiss your eyes—I remember that then I tasted the salt in my mouth and that the tear salt in your eyes was my love for you. But what had even more wrapped me in a fright of love had been, in the depths of the depths of the salt, your bland, innocent, childish substance: in exchange for my kiss your more deeply insipid life was given me, and kissing your face was bland, busy, patient love-work, it was a woman weaving a man, just as you had woven me, the neutral artisanry of life."

Neutral artisanry of life.

My having kissed, for a whole day, the tasteless residue in tear salt made the room's unfamiliarity recognizable, like already-experienced matter. If I had not recognized it till then, it was because it had been only blandly experienced by my deepest bland blood. I recognized everything's familiarity. The figures on the wall I recognized with a new way of looking. And I also recognized the cockroach's vigil. The cockroach's vigil was life living, my own vigilant life living itself out.

I felt in my robe pockets, found a cigarette and matches, lit it.

In the sun the white mass on the cockroach was becoming dryer and slightly yellowed. That told me that more time had passed than I had imagined. A cloud covered the sun for an instant, and I suddenly saw the same room sunless.

Not dark, just lightless. I then perceived that the room existed in itself, that it wasn't just the sun's heat, it could also be cold and calm like the moon. Imagining what its moonlit night might be like, I breathed in deeply, as though I had entered a calm backwater. Even though I also knew that the cold moon wasn't the room either. The room was a thing in itself. It was the high monotony of a breathing eternity. That intimidated me. The world would not intimidate me only if I became the world. If I am the world I won't be afraid. If one is the world, one is directed by a delicate, guiding radar.

When the cloud passed, the sun became clearer and whiter in the room.

Once in a while, in the flick of a second, the cockroach would flutter its antennae. Its eyes kept looking at me monotonously, the two neutral, fertile ovaries. In them I recognized my own two anonymous neutral ovaries. And I didn't want to, oh how I didn't want to!

I had taken the telephone off the hook, but someone might come ring the doorbell and I would be free! The blouse! the blouse I bought, they said they were going to deliver it, so the bell would ring!

No, it wouldn't ring. And I would be forced to keep on with my realizations. And I recognized in the cockroach the insipidity of when I was pregnant.

"I remembered myself walking the streets when I realized that I would have the abortion, doctor, I who as regards children only knew and only would know that I would have an abortion. But at least I was experiencing pregnancy. On the street, I could feel inside myself the child not yet moving, while I stopped to look at the wax manikins smiling in the shop windows. And when I went into the restaurant and ate, a child's pores devoured the food like a waiting fish mouth. When I walked, when I walked, I was carrying it."

In the interminable hours when I walked through the streets thinking about the abortion, which had anyway already been arranged with you, doctor, in those hours my eyes too must have been insipid. On the street I too was no more than thousands of neutral protozoan cilia, quavering, I now knew within myself the shiny stare of a cockroach pinned at the middle. I had walked through the streets with my lips parched, and living, doctor, was the inside of a crime. Pregnancy: I had been cast into the happy horror of neutral life that lives and moves.

And while I was looking into the display windows, doctor, with my dried lips like someone's who isn't breathing through his nose, while I was looking at the stationary, smiling manikins, I was full of neutral plankton and opened my quiet, suffocated mouth and said this to you: "What bothers me most, doctor, is that I have a hard time breathing." The plankton gave me my color, the Tapajós River is green because its plankton is green.

When night arrived, I was still deliberating about the abortion that had been decided on, lying on the bed with my thousands of faceted eyes looking into the dark, my lips dark from breathing, without thinking, without thinking, deliberating, deliberating: on those nights I would gradually darken through and through from my own plankton, just as the cockroach matter was becoming yellower and yellower, and my gradual darkening marked time's passing. And could all of that have been love for the child?

If it was, then love is much more than love: love is yet before love: it is plankton striving, and the great living neutrality striving. Just like life inside the cockroach pinned around the middle.

The fear I have always had of the silence that life is made up of. Fear of the neutral. The neutral was my deepest, most alive root—I looked at the cockroach and I knew. Till the moment I saw the cockroach, I had always given what I was experiencing some name, if I hadn't given it one I couldn't have saved myself. To escape from the neutral, I had long since abandoned the being for the persona, for the human mask. In humanizing myself, I had freed myself from the desert.

I had freed myself from the desert, to be sure, but I had also missed it! And I had also missed the forests, and I had missed the air, and I had missed the embryo inside me.

There it is nevertheless, this neutral cockroach without a name for love or suffering. Its only differentiation in life is that it has to be either male or female. I had been thinking of it only as female since whatever is caved in at the middle must be female.

I put out the cigarette butt that was now burning my fingers, I put it out carefully on the floor with my slipper, and I crossed my sweaty legs, I never thought that legs could sweat so much. We two, the buried alive. If I was brave, I would wipe the sweat off the cockroach.

Did she sense something in herself equivalent to what my gaze saw in her? how much did she do herself any good or get any benefit from what she was? did she know, at least in some indirect way, that she scraped along the ground? or isn't scraping along the ground something that one knows one is doing? How much did I know of what people saw clearly in me? How would I know whether I did or did not go about with my belly dragging in the dust of the ground? Does the truth have no witness? is to be not to know? If a person doesn't look and doesn't see, does the truth still exist? The truth that is not communicated, not even to the one who is looking. Is that the secret of a person's being a person?

If I want to, even now after everything that has happened is over, I can still keep myself from having seen. And then I shall never know about the truth I am trying to go through again—it still depends on me!

I was looking around at the dry, white room, where I saw only sands and more sands of the demolition, some covering over the others. The minaret where I stood was made of hard gold. I was on the hard, unreceptive gold. And I needed to be received. I was afraid.

"Mother: I have taken a life, and there are no arms to receive me now and in the hour of our desert, amen. Mother, everything has now turned into hard gold. I have cut off an organized thing, Mother, and that is worse than killing, that has made me come in through a gap that offered itself to me, worse than death, that showed me a whole, neutral life, yellowing. The cockroach is alive, and its eye fecundates, I am afraid of my raucousness, Mother."

And my mute raucousness was by then the raucousness of someone who is availing herself of a calm Hell.

Raucousness — on the part of someone experiencing pleasure. Hell was good for me, I was taking advantage of that white blood I had spilled. The cockroach is real, Mother. It isn't just the idea of a cockroach anymore.

"Mother, I only pretended to want to kill, but just see what I have cracked: I have cracked a shell! Killing is also forbidden because you crack the hard husk and you are left with viscous life. From the inside of the husk, a heart that is thick and white and living, like pus, comes out, Mother, blessed be you among cockroaches, now and in the hour of this, my death of yours, cockroach and jewel."

As if saying the word "Mother" had released a thick, white part in me — the oratorio's intense resonance suddenly stopped, and the minaret fell silent. And, like after a violent attack of vomiting, my forehead was relieved, fresh, and cool. No more fear, not even fright anymore.

No more fear, not even fright anymore.

Had I vomited up my last human remnants? And I wasn't looking for help anymore. The day desert lay before me. And now the oratorio started in again only in a different way, now the oratorio was the deaf sound of the heat refracting off the walls and ceilings, off the round ceiling vault. The oratorio was made of the trembling of a heat wave. And my fear, too, was different now: not the fear of someone who is still about to go in but the so much greater fear of someone who has gone in.

So much greater: it was fear of my lack of fear.

For it was with my temerity that I then looked at the cockroach. And I saw: it was an insect without beauty in the eyes of other species. And when I looked at it, there the old, small fear came back for just an instant: "I swear, I shall do everything you want! but don't leave me trapped in the cockroach's room because a huge thing is going to happen to me, I don't like the other species! I like only people!

But, when I moved slightly backward, the oratorio only grew more intense, and then I remained silent without attempting another move to help myself. I had now abandoned myself—I could almost see, there at the start of the path I had just traveled, the body I had left behind. But I still called to it now and again, still called myself. And it was when I couldn't hear my reply anymore that I knew that I had finally left myself beyond my own reach.

Yes, the cockroach was an insect without beauty in the eyes of the other species. Its mouth: if it had teeth they would be huge teeth, square and yellow. How I hate the sunlight that shows all, shows even the possible. I wiped my forehead with the corner of my robe, without taking my eyes off the cockroach, and my own eyes too had the same lashes. But no one touches yours, oh filthy one. Only another cockroach would like this cockroach.

And me—who would like me this day? who had become as mute as I? who, like me, was calling fear love? and wanting, love? and needing, love? Who, like me, knew that she had never changed shape since the time when they drew me on the cave rock? beside a man and a dog.

From now on I could call anything the name I invented for it: in the dry room one could do that, for any name would do since none would do. Within the dry vault sounds, everything could be called anything, because anything would be changed into the same resonating muteness. The cockroach's much greater nature made anything that came in there—name or person—lose its false transcendence. As soon as I saw, only and precisely, the white vomit of its body: I saw only facts and things. I knew I was at the point of irreducibility, although I didn't know what the irreducible was.

But I also knew that ignorance of the law of irreducibility was no excuse. I could no longer excuse myself with the claim that I didn't know the law—for knowledge of self and of the world is the law that, even though unattainable, cannot be broken, and no one can excuse himself by saying that he doesn't know it. Worse: the cockroach and I were not in the presence of a law to which we owed obedience. The renewed originality of the sin is this: I have to carry out my own unknown law, and if I don't carry out my unknowing, I shall be sinning originally against life.

In the Garden of Eden, who was the monster and who was not? amid the buildings and apartments, in the elevated spaces between the skyscrapers, in that hanging garden . . . who is, and who is not? To what extent can I stand not at least knowing what is staring at me? the primal cockroach is staring at me, and its law sees mine. I sensed that I was going to know.

"Don't leave me at this moment, don't let me make alone this already-made decision. I had, indeed I still had the desire to take refuge in my own fragility and in the clever, though true, argument that my shoulders were those of a woman, thin and weak. Whenever I had needed to, I had excused myself with the argument that I was a woman. But I understood well that not only women fear seeing, everyone fears seeing him who is God."

I was afraid of God's face, I was afraid of my final nakedness on the wall. The beauty, that new absence of beauty that had nothing to do with what I had been in the habit of calling beauty, terrified me.

"Give me your hand. For I no longer know what I am speaking of. I think I have invented it all, none of it has existed! But if I invented what happened to me yesterday—who can assure me that I didn't also make up my whole life prior to yesterday?"

Give me your hand:

Give me your hand:

Now I'm going to tell you how I went into that inexpressiveness that was always my blind, secret quest. How I went into what exists between the number one and the number two, how I saw the mysterious, fiery line, how it is a surreptitious line. Between two musical notes there exists another note, between two facts there exists another fact, between two grains of sand, no matter how close together they are, there exists an interval of space, there exists a sensing between sensing—in the interstices of primordial matter there is the mysterious, fiery line that is the world's breathing, and the world's continual breathing is what we hear and call silence.

It wasn't by using any of my attributes as an instrument that I was reaching the mysterious, calm fire of that something that is a plasma—it was precisely by stripping myself of all attributes and going on with just my living innards. To arrive at that point, I was leaving my human organization behind—in order to go into that monstrous thing that is my living neutrality.

"I know, it's awful to hold my hand. It's awful to go without air in this collapsed mine into which I have brought you, without pity for you but because of pity for myself. But I swear that I shall get you out of here alive — even if I have to lie, even if I have to lie about what my eyes have seen. I'll save you from this terror in which, for the moment, I need you. What pity I now have for you, a person I have simply latched on to. You gave me your hand innocently, and because I could hold on to it I have had the courage to plunge to the depths of myself. But don't try to understand me, just keep me company. I know that your hand would let go if you knew."

How can I repay you? At least use me too, at least use me as a dark tunnel . . . and when you walk through my blackness you will come out the other side with yourself. You may not come out with me, I don't know if I'll go through, but you'll come out with yourself. At least you won't be alone, like I was yesterday, and yesterday I prayed just to get out from inside alive. And not only alive — like that primary, monstrous cockroach was only alive — but organizedly alive, like a person.

Identity — identity which is the first immanence — was that what I was giving in to? was that what I had gone into?

Identity is forbidden me, I know. But I am going to put myself at peril by having faith in my future cowardice, and it will be my essential cowardice that will reorganize me again into a person.

Not only through my cowardice. But I shall reorganize myself through the ritual with which I have now been born, just as the ritual of life is inherent in the neutrality of semen. Identity is forbidden me but my love is so great that I shall not resist my will to go into the mysterious web, into that plasma that I may never be able to leave. My belief, however, is also so profound that, if I cannot leave, I know, even in my new unreality, there will be the plasma of God in my life.

Oh, but at the same time, how can I want my heart to see? if my body is so weak that I cannot look at the sun without my eyes physically weeping—how could I keep my heart from shining in physically organic tears if in nakedness I felt identity: God? My heart, which has cloaked itself in a thousand veils.

The great, neutral reality of what I was experiencing outstripped me in its extreme objectivity. I felt unable to be as real as the reality that was reaching me—could I be starting in contortions to be as nakedly real as what I was seeing? However, I experienced all this reality with a sense of the unreality of reality. Could I be living not truth but the myth of truth? Whenever I experienced truth, it was through an impression of unshakable dream: unshakable dream is my truth.

I am trying to tell you how I came to the neutrality and inexpressivity of myself. I don't know if I am understanding what I say, I feel—and I very much fear feeling, for feeling is merely one of the styles of being. Still, I shall go through the sultry torpor that swells with nothingness, and I shall have to understand neutrality through feeling.

Neutrality. I am speaking of the vital element linking things. Oh, I'm not afraid you won't understand but rather that I'll understand myself poorly. If I don't understand myself, I shall die of exactly what I'm still living on. Let me now tell you the most frightening part:

I was being swept along by the demonic.

For the unexpressive is diabolical. If a person is not committed to hope, she lives in the demonic. If that person has the courage to leave her feeling behind, she discovers that huge life of an extremely busy silence, the same sort that exists in the cockroach, the same as in the stars, the same as in herself—the demonic is *prior* to the human. And if that person sees that nowness, she singes herself, as though she saw God. Prehuman divine life is a life of singeing nowness.

Prehuman divine life is a life of singeing nowness.

I am going to tell you: the fact is that I was afraid of a certain blind and now fierce joy that began to take me over. And to make me lose myself.

The joy of losing oneself is a Black Sabbath joy. Losing oneself is finding oneself dangerous. I was experiencing in that desert the fire of things: and it was a neutral fire. I was living off the whole span that things comprise. And it was a Hell, that experience, because in that world that I was living there exists neither pity nor hope.

I had come into the Sabbath orgy. I know now what is done in the darkness of the mountains during nights of orgy. I know! I know with horror: things are enjoyed. The thing of which things are made is delighted in—that is the brute joy of black magic. It was that neutrality that I experienced—neutrality was my true cultural broth. I kept going on, and I was feeling the joy of Hell.

And Hell is not the torture of pain! it is the torture of a certain joy.

The neutral is unexplainable and alive, it seeks to understand me: just as protoplasm and semen and protein belong to a living neutrality. And I was completely new, like a new initiate. It was as if up to now I had had my palate corrupted by salt and sugar, my soul corrupted by pleasures and pains—and I had never tasted the primary taste. And I now experienced the taste of nothingness. I quickly uncorrupted myself, and the taste was new like the taste of mother's milk that has a taste only to the mouth of the child. With the collapse of my culture and my humanity—which was a suffering with a great sense of loss for me—with the loss of humanity, I came, orgiastically, to taste the taste of things' identity.

It is very hard to taste. Up to then I had been so swollen with feeling that when I experienced the taste of real identity, it seemed as tasteless as the taste that a drop of rainwater has in your mouth. It's horribly insipid, my love.

My love, it's like the blandest nectar—it's like the air, which in itself has no smell at all. Up to then, my corrupted senses were mute to the taste of things. But my most archaic and demonic of thirsts had led me, subterraneously, to collapse all constructs. Sinful thirst was guiding me—and I know now that tasting the taste of that almost-nothingness is the gods' secret joy. It is a nothingness that is God—and that has no taste.

But it is the most primary of pleasures. And only it—at last, at last!—is the pole opposite to the pole of Christian-human feeling. Through the pole of the first demonic pleasure I perceived, at a great distance and for the first time . . . that there really was an opposite pole.

I was clear of my own intoxication by feelings, clear to the point of going into the divine life that was a primary life entirely without elegance, a life as primary as if it was a manna falling from the heavens without any taste whatsoever: manna is like rain and has no taste. To taste that taste of nothingness was my condemnation and my joyful terror.

Oh, my unknown love, remember that I was trapped there in the caved-in mine and that by then the room had taken on an unexpressible familiarity, like the familiar honesty of dreams. And, just as in dreams, what I can't recount for you is the atmosphere's essential color. Like in dreams, the "logic" was other, was one that makes no sense when you wake up, for the dream's greater truth is lost.

But remember that all this took place while I was awake and immobilized by the daylight, and the dream truth was taking place without the anesthesia of night. Sleep awake along with me, and only then will you be able to know of my great sleep and know what the living desert is like.

Suddenly, as I was sitting there, a fatigue completely rigid, with no lassitude in it, came over me. Any more and it would have petrified me.

Then, carefully, as though some parts of me were paralyzed, I lay down on the rough mattress and there, burned through and through, I went to sleep as immediately as a cockroach goes to sleep on a vertical wall. There was no human stability in my sleep: it was the kind of balance a cockroach has when it sleeps on the whitewashed surface of a wall.

When I awoke, there was an even whiter and more fervidly fixed sun in the room. After that sleep, to the dimensionless surface of which my feet had clung, I was now trembling with cold.

But then the numbness passed, and again, fully in the sun's heat, I suffocated in confinement.

It must be past noon. I got up before I had really decided to and, even though it was useless, tried to throw open even wider the already fully opened window, and I tried to breathe, even though it might be breathing from a visual vastness, I sought a vastness.

I sought a vastness.

From that room dug out of the rock of a building, from the window of my minaret, I saw all the way to the horizon the enormous expanse of roof after roof calmly parching in the sun. The apartment buildings, like villages, crouched on their haunches. In size, it was larger than Spain.

Beyond the rocky defiles, between the concrete of the buildings, I saw the *favela* on the hilltop, and I saw a goat slowly walking up the hill. Beyond, there extended the plains of Asia Minor. From there I contemplated the empire of the present. The strait of the Dardanelles was farther over there; beyond it the craggy peaks. Your majestic monotony. Your imperial expanse, there in the sun.

And beyond, the sands began. The naked, burning desert. When darkness fell, cold would consume the desert, and one would shiver there like on desert nights. But in the distance the salty blue lake shimmered. That, then, must be the region of the great salt lakes.

Under the tremulous waves of sultry heat, monotony. Through the other apartment windows and on the concrete balconies, I saw the activity of shadows and people, like the comings and goings of the first Assyrian merchants. They were fighting for control of Asia Minor.

Perhaps I had excavated the future—or had got through to ancient profundities coming from so far away that my hands that had unearthed them could not even suspect. There I was, on foot, like a child dressed in a habit, a sleepy child. But an inquisitive child. From the height of this building, the present contemplates the present. Just as in the second millennium before Christ.

And I, now I was no longer an inquisitive child. I had grown, and I had become as simple as a queen. Kings, sphinxes, and lions, behold the city where I live—and all extinct! I am left over, pinned down by one of the stones that fell. And, since silence has judged my motionlessness to be that of a dead person, they all forgot me, left without getting me out, and, considered dead, I have stayed here, watching. And I have seen, while the silence of those who had really died kept invading me like ivy grows into the mouths of stone lions.

And because I was sure that I would end up starving to death under the fallen stone that pinned down my limbs . . . I saw like someone who is never going to tell. I saw with the lack of commitment of someone who is not even going to tell herself. I saw very like someone who will never need to understand what she saw. Just as a lizard's nature sees: without ever having to remember. The lizard sees—like a loose eye sees.

I may have been the first person to set foot in that castle in the air. Five million years ago, perhaps the last caveman looked out from this very place, where there could then have been a mountain here. And which, after it had worn down, later became an empty place where, still later, cities were built that had worn away in their turn. Today the ground is fully populated by diverse races.

Standing at the window, sometimes my eyes rested on the blue lake that may have been nothing more than a piece of sky. But it soon wore me out, for the blue was made of a great intensity of light. My bleary eyes then shifted to rest on the naked, burning desert, which at least did not have the hardness of a color. Three millennia from now, hidden oil would gush from those sands: the present was opening gigantic perspectives on a new present.

In the meantime, today, I lived in the silence of what three millennia from now, after it had worn away and had been raised again, would again be stairs, cranes, men, and buildings. I was living the prehistory of a future. Like a woman who never had children but would have them three millennia from now, I was living today on the oil that would gush forth in those three millennia.

If at least I had come into the room at sundown — tonight would still be a full moon, I remembered that when I recalled the party on the balcony last night — I would see the full moon being born over the desert.

"Oh, I want to go back to my home," I suddenly entreated myself, for the moist moon had made me yearn for my life. But from that platform I got no moment of darkness and moon. Only hot coals, only the errant wind. And for me no canteen of water, no pipe of food.

But, who knows, less than a year later I might make such a find as no one, not even myself, would have dared predict. A golden chalice?

For I was looking for my city's treasure.

A city of gold and stone, Rio de Janeiro, whose inhabitants in the sun were six hundred thousand beggars. The city's treasure might be in one of the breaches in the rubble. But which one? That city was in need of a mapmaker.

As I lifted my gaze to ever more distant points, to even steeper heights, there arose before me gigantic blocks of buildings that formed a heavy design, one not yet shown on any maps. I continued with that gaze, sought on the hill the remains of some fortified wall. After they reached the top of the hill I let my eyes run over the panorama. I mentally traced a circle around the semiruins of the *favelas*, and I realized that a city as large and limpid as Athens at its zenith could once have lived there, with children running through merchandise set out along the streets.

My way of seeing was entirely impartial: I worked directly with the evidence of my sight, without letting suggestions other than visual ones predetermine my conclusions; I was wholly prepared to surprise myself. Even if the evidence should contradict what I had decided on in my most tranquil delirium.

I know — through my own personal witness — that at the outset of this search of mine I hadn't the slightest idea what kind of language would slowly be revealed to me until I could one day reach Constantinople. But now I was totally prepared to bear in this room the hot, humid season of our climate, and with it, cobras, scorpions, tarantulas, and hordes of mosquitoes that come out when a city is demolished. And I knew that often, in my work in the open air, I would have to share my bed with the animals.

Meanwhile the sun was scorching me through the window. Only today had the sun hit me full on. But it was also true that only when the sun hit me could I myself, by standing up, be a source of shade — in which I would keep fresh skins of my water.

I was going to need a drill twelve meters long, camels, goats, and sheep, an electric cable; and I was going to need direct use of the vastness itself, for it would be impossible to reproduce, for example, in a simple aquarium, the richness of the oxygen found on ocean surfaces.

To keep my work spirit from flagging, I would try not to forget that geologists now know that in the Sahara's subsoil there is a huge lake of potable water, I remember reading that; and that in the Sahara itself archaeologists have already excavated remnants of household utensils and the remains of ancient settlements: seven thousand years ago, I had read, a prosperous agriculture had developed in that "region of fear." The desert has a humidity that must be found again.

How should I proceed? to hold down the sand dunes, I would have to plant two million green trees, especially eucalyptus trees—I have always had the habit of reading something before going to sleep, and I had read a lot about the properties of eucalyptus trees.

And I must not forget, at the start of the work, to be prepared to make mistakes. Not forget that mistakes had often proved to be my path. Every time what I thought or felt didn't work out . . . a space would somehow open up, and if I had had the courage before I would have gone in through it. But I had always been afraid of delirium and error. My error, however, had to be the path of truth: for only when I err do I get away from what I know and what I understand. If "truth" were what I can understand . . . it would end up being but a small truth, my-sized.

Truth must reside precisely in what I shall never understand. And would I then be able to understand myself afterward? I don't know. Will the man of the future understand us as we are today? He, with distracted tenderness, will distractedly pat our heads like we do with a dog who comes up to us and looks at us from within its darkness, with silent, stricken eyes. He, the future man, would pat us, remotely comprehending us, just as I would remotely understand myself afterward, with the memory of the memory of the long-lost memory of a time of pain, but knowing that our time of pain would pass, just as a child is not a static child but a growing being.

All right, after holding the sand dunes down with eucalyptus trees, I couldn't forget, if it came up, that rice prospers in brackish soil, the high salt content of which it helps to cut down; that too I remembered from the bedtime reading that I tried to keep impersonal so it would help me fall asleep.

And what other tools would I need to dig with? picks, a hundred and fifty shovels, winches, even though I didn't know exactly what a winch was, heavy carts with steel axles, a portable forge, as well as nails and cord. As for my hunger, for my hunger I would make use of the dates of ten million palm trees, as well as peanuts and olives. And I had to know beforehand that, at prayer time in my minaret, I could only pray for the sands.

But for the sands I had probably been ready since I was born: I would know how to pray them, for that I wouldn't need to train myself ahead of time, like the witch doctors who do not pray *for* things but pray things. Prepared I had always been, so trained had I been by fear.

I remembered what was engraved in my memory, and up to that moment, uselessly: that Arabs and nomads call the Sahara El Khela, nothing, call it Tanesruft, the country of fear, call it Tiniri, land beyond the pasture regions. To pray the sands, I, like they, had already been prepared by fear.

Once again too scorched, I sought the great blue lakes, where I submerged my dried-out eyes. Lakes or luminous spots of sky. The lakes were neither ugly nor pretty. And it was only that that still terrorized my humanity. I tried to think about the Black Sea, I tried to think about the Persians coming down through the passes . . . but in all this too I found neither beauty nor ugliness, just the infinite successions of centuries of the world.

Which, suddenly, I could no longer tolerate.

And I suddenly turned back to the inside of the room, which, in its oppressiveness, at least was unpopulated.

I suddenly turned back to the inside of the room, which, in its oppressiveness, at least was unpopulated.

No, in all of this I had not been crazy or out of control. It was just a visual meditation. The danger of meditation is the danger of starting to think without wanting to, and thinking is no longer meditating, thinking leads toward an objective. Less dangerous is to "see" in meditation, which bypasses words of thought. I know that there now exists an electron microscope that gives the image of an object a hundred and sixty thousand times greater than actual size . . . but I wouldn't call the sight that one gets through that microscope hallucinatory, even though the small object that it has so monstrously magnified is no longer identifiable.

Had I deluded myself in my visual meditation?

Absolutely probable. But also in my purely optical visions, of a chair or a pitcher, I am the victim of error: my visual witness of a pitcher or of a chair is faulty at various points. The error is the error of my unalterable work methods.

I sat down on the bed again. But now, looking at the cockroach, I knew much more.

Looking at it, I saw the vastness of the Libyan desert, in the area of Elschele. The cockroach that had preceded me there by millennia, and also preceded the dinosaurs. In the presence of the cockroach, I was now able to see to far-off Damascus, the oldest city on earth. On the Libyan desert, cockroaches and crocodiles? All the time I had been wanting not to think about what I was really thinking now: that the cockroach is edible like a lobster, the cockroach was a crustacean.

And I have only loathing for crocodiles' crawling since I am not a crocodile. I have a horror of the crocodile's silence, full of rows of scales.

But the loathing is necessary for me just as water pollution is necessary for what is in the water to reproduce. Loathing directs me and makes me fertile. Through loathing I see a night in Galilee. The night in Galilee is as if the vastness of the desert walked in the darkness. The cockroach is a dark vastness walking.

I was now living the Hell through which I was still to pass, but I did not know if it would be passage through or if I would remain there. I knew now that that Hell is horrible and is good, perhaps I would want to stay in it. For I was seeing the profound, ancient life of the cockroach. I was seeing a silence that has the depth of an embrace. The sun is as much in the Libyan desert as it is hot in itself. And the earth is the sun, how is it that I never saw before that the earth is the sun?

And then there will take place—on a naked, dry rock in the Libyan desert—there will take place the love of two cockroaches. And now I know what it is like. One cockroach waits. I see its brown-thing silence. And now—now I see another cockroach advancing slowly and with difficulty through the sands toward the rock. Upon the rock, which had had its body of water dry up millennia ago, two dry cockroaches. One is the silence of the other. The killers who face each other: the world is utterly reciprocal. An entirely mute stridulation vibrating atop the rock; and we, we who have come down to today, still resonate with it.

"I promise myself for one day this same silence, I promise us what I have now learned. Only for us it will have to be by night, for we are moist, salty beings, we are beings of sea water and of tears. It will also be with cockroaches' wholly open eyes, except that it will be in the night, for I am a creature of great, moist depths, I do not know the dust of dry cisterns, and the surface of a rock is not my hearth."

We are creatures who need to dive to the depths in order there to breathe, like fish dive in the water to breathe, only for me the depths are in the night air. The night is our latent state. And it is so moist that plants are born there. In houses the lights are put out so the crickets can be heard more clearly and so that the grasshoppers may move across the leaves almost without touching them, the leaves, the leaves, the leaves—in the night soft anxiousness is transmitted through the air's hollowness, emptiness is a medium of transport.

Yes indeed, for us love will not be on the daytime desert: we are those who swim, the night air is humid and is sweetened, and we are salty since our breathing-out is sweat. A long time ago I was drawn, along with you, on a cave wall, and with you I have swum from its dark depths down to today, I have swum with my countless cilia—I was the oil that just today gushed forth, when a black African drew me in my own house, making me come forth from a wall. Sleepwalking, like the oil that finally gushes forth.

"I swear that love is like that. I know, only because I was sitting there and I found out. Only because of the cockroach do I know that all that the two of us had before was already love. What had to happen was for the cockroach to hurt me like someone pulling out my fingernails—and then I couldn't stand the torture any longer and I confessed, and now I am telling it all. I could stand no more and I confess that I already knew of a truth that never had use and application, and that I would be afraid to apply, for I am not adult enough to be able to use a truth without destroying myself."

If you can find out through me, without having to be tortured first, without first having to be cut in half by a wardrobe door, without first having your shells broken, shells of fear that through time had been hardening into shells of stone, just as mine had to be broken under a pincers' force until I reached the tender neutrality of myself—if you can find out through me . . . then learn from this one who has had to be laid completely bare and lose all her suitcases with the engraved initials.

"Plumb me, plumb me, for it is cold, it is cold to lose your lobstershells. Warm me with your plumbing, comprehend me, for I do not comprehend myself. I am just in love with the cockroach. And it is a Hellish love."

But you are afraid, I know that you were always afraid of rituals. But when one is tortured until she becomes a nucleus, then one changes demonically to wanting to serve ritual, even if the ritual is the act of self-consumption—just as for there to be incense one must burn incense. Listen, because I am as serious as a cockroach with cilia. Listen:

When a person is her own nucleus, she can have no more disparities. Then she is her own solemnity and no longer fears self-consumption in the service of consuming ritual—ritual is the very life of the nucleus carrying itself out, the ritual is not outside it: the ritual is inherent. The cockroach has its ritual within its cell. Ritual—believe in me because I think I understand now—ritual is the mark of

God. And every child is born with the same ritual already there.

"I know: the two of us were always afraid of my solemnity and of your solemnity. We thought it was a solemnity of form. And we always hid what we knew: that living is always a question of life and death, hence the solemnity. We knew too, albeit without the gift of the grace of knowing it, that we are the life that is inside us, and that we do for ourselves. The only destiny with which we are born is the destiny of ritual. I have been calling "mask" a lie, and it isn't: it is the essential mask of solemnity. We would have to put on ritual masks to love each other. Beetles are born with the mask with which they will fulfill themselves. Through original sin we have lost our mask."

I looked; the cockroach was a beetle. It was merely its own mask. In the cockroach's lack of glee I perceived its warrior ferocity. It was meek but its functioning was fierce.

I am meek but *my* life-function is fierce. Oh, pre-human love invades me. I understand, I understand! The form of living is so secret a secret that it is the silent tracking of a secret. It is a secret in the desert. I knew for certain now. For in the light of two cockroaches' love there came to me the memory of a true love that I once had and didn't know that I had—for love was then what I understood from a word. But there is something that must be said, that must be said.

But there is something that must be said, that must be said.

"I am going to tell you what I have never told you before, maybe that's what's missing: to have told. If I didn't tell, it wasn't because I begrudged telling or because of my cockroach silence with more eyes than mouth. If I didn't tell, it was because I didn't know that I knew—but I know now. I am going to tell you that I love you. I know that I have said that to you before and that it was true when I said it then as well, but only now am I really saying it. I need to say it before I . . . . Oh, but it is the cockroach that is going to die, not me! I don't need this condemned person's letter from a cell . . . "

"No, I don't want to frighten you with my love. If you become frightened of me, I'll become frightened of myself. Don't be afraid of the pain. I am now as sure as I am sure that in that room I was alive and the cockroach was alive: I am sure of this: that everything happens above or below pain. Pain isn't the true name of what people call pain. Listen: I'm sure of this."

For, now that I was not struggling with myself any longer, I quietly knew that that's what a cockroach was like, that pain wasn't pain.

Oh, if I had known what was going to happen in the room I'd have picked up more cigarettes before I came in: I was consuming myself in the need to smoke.

"Oh, if only I could transmit to you the memory, just now brought to life, of what we two have experienced without knowing it. Do you want to remember along with me? oh, I know that it's hard: but let's reach out for ourselves. Instead of going beyond ourselves. Don't be afraid now, you're safe because at least it has already happened—unless you see some danger in knowing that it happened."

The fact is that when we were in love I didn't know that love happened much more precisely when there was no what we then called love. The neuter of love, that is what we were experiencing, and what we rejected.

What I am talking about is when nothing was happening, and we called that nothing an interval. How could it have been an interval?

It was the huge flower opening up, all full of itself, my vision all huge and tremulous. What I saw then came together to my sight and became mine—but not a permanent coming-together: if I had compressed it between my hands like a piece of coagulated blood, its solidity would have turned back into liquid blood again between my fingers.

And time wasn't totally liquid only because, for me to be able to pick things up with my hands, the things had to coagulate, the way fruits hold together. In the intervals that we called empty and tranquil, and when we thought that the love had ended . . .

I remember my throat pains back then: with my swollen tonsils, I had quick coagulation. And it melted easily: my throat pain had gone away, I used to find myself telling you. Like iceflows in the summer and the rivers running liquid. Every word of ours—in that time that we called empty—every word was as light and empty as a butterfly: the inner word fluttered against the mouth, the words were said but we didn't hear them because the melted iceflows made a great deal of noise when they ran. In the midst of the roar of liquid, our mouths moved, speaking, and we really only saw the mouths moving but we didn't hear them—we looked into each other's mouth, seeing it speak, and it mattered little that we didn't hear, oh, in God's name, it mattered little.

And in our own name, it was enough just to see the mouth speaking, and we laughed because we paid little attention. And we nevertheless called that not-hearing disinterest and lack of love.

But, really, how we did speak! we spoke nothingness. Yet everything shimmered like when heavy tears cling to eyes; therefore, everything shimmered.

In those intervals we used to think that we were relaxing from one being the other. In fact, it was the great pleasure of not being the other: for in that case we each were two. Everything would end when what we called our interval in love ended; and, because it was going to end, it weighed tremulously with the very weight of its end already in itself. I remember all that as though through a trembling in water.

Oh, could it be that we were not originally human? and that we became human through practical necessity? that terrifies me, just as it does you. For the cockroach looked at me with her beetle shell, with her burst body all made of tubes and antennae and soft cement—and that was undeniably a truth prior to our words, it was undeniably the life that up to then I hadn't wanted.

"Then—then, through the door of condemnation, I ate life and was eaten by life. I understood that my kingdom is of this world. And I understood it through the Hellish side of me. For within myself I saw what Hell is like."

For within myself I saw what Hell is like.

Hell is the mouth that bites and eats living flesh that has blood, and the one eaten howls with delight in his eye: Hell is the pain like pleasure of matter, and with the laughter of delight tears run in pain. And the tear that comes from pain's laughter is the opposite of redemption. I could see the cockroach's inexorability with her ritual mask. I saw that Hell was just that: cruel acceptance of pain, solemn lack of pity for one's own destiny, love of the ritual of life more than oneself—that was Hell, where the one who ate the living flesh of the other wallowed about in the happiness of pain.

For the first time I felt with Hellish greed the wish to have borne the children I never had: I wanted my organic Hellishness full of pleasure to have reproduced itself not in three or four offspring but in twenty thousand. My future survival in offspring would be my true nowness, which is not only myself but my pleasureful species not losing its continuity. Not having borne offspring left me spasmodic, as though I were confronting a vice I had rejected.

That cockroach had had children and I had not: the cockroach could die squashed, but I was condemned never to die, for if I died, albeit only once, I would die. And I wanted not to die but to keep perpetually dying like a supreme pleasure in pain. I was in the Hell traversed by pleasure like a very low nerve-buzz of pleasure.

And all that—oh, my horror—all that took place in the immense refuge of indifference. . . . All that losing itself in a spiraling destiny, and that destiny not losing itself. In that infinite destiny made only of cruel nowness, I, like a larva—in my deepest inhumanity, for what had up to now escaped me had been my real inhumanity—I and we as larvae devour each other in soft flesh.

And there is no punishment! Hell is that; there is no punishment. For in Hell we make what could be punishment into supreme delight, in this desert we make punishment into one more ecstasy of laughter with tears, in Hell we make punishment into an expectation of pleasure.

Was this, then, the other side of humanization and of hope?

In Hell that demonic faith for which I am not responsible. And which is faith in orgiastic life. Hell's orgy is the apotheosis of the neutral. Black Sabbath joy is the joy of losing oneself in the atonal.

What still frightened me was that even that very unpunishable horror would be benignly reabsorbed into the abyss of endless time, into the abyss of unending heights, into the profound abyss of God: absorbed into the core of an indifference.

So different from human indifference. For it was an interested indifference, an attainable indifference. It was an extremely energetic indifference. And all is silence in that Hell of mine. For the laughter forms part of the volume of the silence, indifferent pleasure gleamed only in the eye, but laughter was in the very blood and can't be heard.

And all this is in this very instant, is in the now. But at the same time the present instant is completely removed because of the immense magnitude of God. Because of that enormous perpetual magnitude, even what exists at the present moment is remote: in the very instant when the cockroach is crushed in the wardrobe, it too is remote in relation to the core of great interested indifference that will reabsorb it with impunity.

Grandiose indifference—was that what existed inside me?

The Hellish immensity of life: for even my body doesn't delimit me, compassion doesn't allow my body to delimit me. In Hell, my body doesn't delimit me, should I call that "soul"? To live a life that is no longer the life of my body . . . should I call that impersonal "soul"?

And my impersonal soul scorches me. A star's grandiose indifference is the cockroach's soul, the star is the very exorbitance of the cockroach's body. The cockroach and I aspire to a peace that cannot be ours—it is a peace beyond her scope and destiny, and mine. And because my soul is so unlimited that it is no longer me, and because it is so beyond me . . . I am always remote from myself, I am unreachable to myself just as a star is unreachable for me. I contort myself to be able to touch the present time that surrounds me, but I remain remote in relation to this very instant itself. The future, God help me, is closer to me than the present instant.

The cockroach and I are Hellishly free because our living matter is greater than we are, we are Hellishly free because my own life is so little containable within my body that I can't even use it. My life is used more by the earth than it is by me, I am so much greater than what I have called "me" that just by having a life of the world I would have myself. It would take a horde of cockroaches to make a minimally perceivable point in the world—however, one lone cockroach, merely because of its life-attention, that lone cockroach *is* the world.

The most unreachable part of my soul, the one not belonging to me, is the part that touches on my border with what is not me and the part to which I give myself over. My whole anxiety has been this untranscendable and excessively close proximity. I am more what is not within me.

And that is why the hand that I was holding has abandoned me. No, no. It was I who let go of the hand, because I now have to go on alone.

If I succeed in returning to the realm of life I shall pick up your hand again, and I shall kiss it in gratitude for its waiting for me, waiting for my sojourn to pass, for me to return, thin, starved, humbled: hungry just for what is little, hungry just for what is less.

Because, sitting here quietly, I have come to want to experience my own remoteness as the only way of experiencing my nowness. And that, which is apparently innocent, that was again an enjoyment that resembled a horrendous, cosmic pleasure.

To relive it, I am letting go of your hand.

Because in that enjoyment there was no pity. Pity is being the offspring of someone or something—but the world's being is cruelty. Cockroaches gnaw each other and kill each other and penetrate each other in procreation and eat each other in an eternal summer that falls into night— Hell is a summer that boils and almost becomes night. Nowness doesn't see the cockroach, present time looks at her from so great a distance that it doesn't make her out from so far away and only sees a silent desert—present time doesn't even suspect the orgiastic gypsy celebration on the naked desert.

Where, reduced to tiny jackals, we eat each other in laughter. In the laughter of pain—and free. The mystery of human destiny is that we are fated, but we have the freedom to fulfill or not fulfill our fate: realization of our fated destiny depends on us. While inhuman beings like the cockroach realize the entire cycle without going astray, because they make no choices. But my freely becoming what I fatefully am depends on me. I am the mistress of my own fatedness, and, if I decide not to complete it, I shall stay outside my specifically living nature. But if I fulfill my neutral, living core, then, within my species, I shall be being specifically human.

"But the fact is that becoming human can become transformed into an ideal, and can suffocate itself through slow accretions . . . . Being human should not be an ideal for humankind, which is human by fate, being human has to be the way I as a living thing obeying through freedom the path of living things, am human. And I don't even need to take care of my soul, it will fatefully take care of me, and I don't need to make a soul for myself: I just have to choose to live. We are free, and this is Hell. But there are so many cockroaches that it seems like a prayer."

My kingdom is of this world . . . my kingdom was not merely human. I knew. But knowing that would spread death-life, and a child in my womb would be threatened with being eaten by that very death-life, and without a Christian word even having meaning . . . But there are so many children in the womb that it seems like a prayer.

At that moment I still had not understood that the first outline of what would be a prayer was already being born from the happy Hell I had gone into and wanted never to leave again.

Never leave that country of rats and tarantulas and cockroaches, my darling, where delight drops in thick drops of blood.

Only God's compassion could pull me away from the terrible, indifferent happiness in which I was bathing, bathing through and through.

For I was exulting. I knew the violence of happy darkness—I was as happy as the Devil, Hell is my maximum.

Hell is my maximum.

I was fully in the harbor of an indifference that is quiet and alert. And in the harbor of an indifferent love, of an indifferent waking sleep, of an indifferent pain. Of a God whom, if I loved, I did not understand what He wanted of me. I know, He wanted me to be His equal, and for me to equal Him through a love I was not capable of.

Through a love so great that it would be love by a person so indifferent . . . as if I were not a human person. He wanted me to be the world with Him. He wanted my human divinity, and that had to start with an initial despoliation of the constructed human being.

And I had taken the first step: for at least I now knew that being human is a sensitizing, an orgasm of nature. And that it is only through an anomaly of nature that, instead of our being God like other beings are, instead of our being Him, we wanted to see Him. It wouldn't be bad to see Him if we were as large as He is. A cockroach is larger than I am because its life is so given over to Him that it comes from the infinite and moves toward the infinite unperceivingly, it never becomes discontinuous.

I had taken the first huge step. But what had happened to me?

I had fallen into the temptation of seeing, into the temptation of knowing and feeling. My grandeur, in search of God's grandeur, had taken me to the grandeur of Hell. I had not been able to understand His organization except through the spasm of a demonic exultation. Curiosity had expelled me from snugness—and I found the indifferent God who is all good because He is neither bad nor good, I was in the harbor of a matter that is the indifferent explosion of itself. Life had the force of a titanic indifference. A titanic indifference that is interested in moving. And I, who wanted to move along with it, I had remained caught by the pleasure that made me merely Hellish.

The temptation of pleasure. The temptation is to partake directly of the source. The temptation is to partake directly of the law. And the punishment is to want never to stop eating, and to eat oneself, for I am likewise edible matter. And I would seek condemnation like a joy. I would seek the most orgiastic part of myself. I would never rest again. I had stolen the hunting horse from a king of joy. I was now worse than my very self!

I would never rest again: I had stolen the hunting horse from the Sabbath king. If I drowse for an instant, the echo of a whinny awakens me. It is useless not to go. In the darkness of night, taking in a deep draught of air gives me the shivers. I pretend to sleep, but in the silence the horse breathes. It says nothing, but it breathes, it waits and breathes. Every day it will be the same thing: right at nightfall I begin to turn melancholy and pensive. I know that the first drum on the mountain will make the night; I know that the third will have already incorporated me in its thunder.

And by the fifth drum I shall already be unconscious of my greed. Until by dawn, by the last, ever-so-light drums, I shall find myself, without knowing how, near a stream, not ever knowing what I have done, beside the enormous, tired horse's head.

Tired from what? What have we done who ride in the Hell of joy? I have not gone out for two centuries. The last time I came down from the enchanted saddle, my human sadness was so great that I swore never to again. The ride, however, continues on in me. I converse, I clean the house, I smile, but I know that the ride is within me. I feel lack, like one who is dying. I can no longer keep from going out.

And I know that at night, when it calls me, I shall go out. I want the horse to lead my thoughts once again. It was from it that I learned. If this hour amid barking is thought. The dogs bark, I begin to grow sad because I know, with my eye now gleaming, that I shall go. When at night it calls me to Hell, I shall go. I go down like a cat upon the roofs. No one knows, no one sees. I offer myself up in the darkness, mute and splendorous. Fifty-three flutes run after us. A clarinet lights our way in front. And nothing more is given me to know.

At dawn I shall see us exhausted near the stream, without knowing what crimes we have committed before the dawn's arrival. In my mouth and on its feet the mark of blood. What have we burned? At dawn I shall be afoot beside the silent horse, with the first bells of a Church running down the stream, with the rest of the flutes still running from my hair.

Night is my life, it grows late, the happy night is my sad life—steal, steal the horse from me because from theft to theft I have stolen even the dawn and made it a foreboding: quickly steal the horse while it's time, while it's not too late, if there is in fact still time, for to steal the horse I had to kill the king and in killing him I have stolen the king's death. And the happiness of the murder consumes me with pleasure.

I was consuming myself, for I too am living matter of the Sabbath.

I was consuming myself, for I too am living matter of the Sabbath.

Could this not be the temptation that the saints went through, albeit much greater? And from which he who would be a saint or not, emerges sanctified or not. Of this temptation on the desert, I, dilettante, unholy, would succumb, or I would emerge from it as for the first time a living being.

"Listen, there exists something that is called human sanctity, and which is not the saints' sanctity. I fear that not even God comprehends that human sanctity is more perilous than divine sanctity, that the sanctity of the dilettante is more painful. Even Christ himself may have known that if they were to do to him what they did, they would do much more to us, for he had said: 'If they have done this to the green bough, what will they do with the dry ones?' "

Proof. Now I understand what proof is. Proof: it means that life is testing me. But proof: it means that I too am proving. And proving can be transformed into an ever more insatiable thirst.

Wait for me: I am going to get you out of the Hell into which I have descended. Listen, listen:

For from my delight without remission there was now being born in me a sobbing that seemed to be one of happiness. They were not sobs of pain, I had never heard them before: they were the sobs of my life dividing to procreate me. On those desert sands I was beginning to be delicate like a first, timid offering, the offering of a flower. What did I offer? what could I offer of myself—I who was the desert, I who had sought and held it?

I offered a sob. I was finally crying within my Hell. The very wings of blackness I use and sweat, and I used and sweated them for myself, for me—for me are You, you, splendor of silence. *I* am not You; *me* are You. For that reason alone will I be able to sense You directly: because You are me.

Oh, God, I was beginning to understand with enormous surprise: my Hellish orgy was human martyrdom itself.

How could I have guessed? if I hadn't known that one laughs when suffering. I just didn't know that one could suffer so. It was then that I called my profoundest suffering happiness.

And God came to me in the sob, God now occupied me through. I offered God my Hell. The first sob had made—of my terrible pleasure and of my celebration—a new pain, which was now as light and helpless as the flower of my own desert. The tears that were now running were like those for a love. God, who could never be understood by me except as I understood Him: breaking me like a flower that on birth can barely raise itself and seems to break on its own.

But now that I knew that suffering had been my happiness, I asked myself if I wasn't fleeing toward a God because I couldn't bear my humanity. For I needed someone who would not be as insignificant as I, someone who would be so much greater than I that he could admit my disgrace without even using pity, and consolation—someone who would be, who would be! and not, like myself, an accuser of nature, and not, like myself, someone frightened by the power of my own hates and loves.

At this moment, now, a doubt overtakes me. God, or whatever You are called: I now ask only one bit of help: but it is that you help me, not in the obscure way in which you are me but now openly, in plain sight.

For I need to know precisely this one thing: am I feeling what I am feeling, or am I feeling what I wanted to feel? or am I feeling what I would need to feel?

Because I no longer want even the concretization of an ideal what I want is to be merely a seed. Even if, after that seed, ideals are born again—be they true ideals, which are births of a path, or false ones, which are mere accretions. Could I be sensing what I would like to sense? For a millimeter's difference is huge, and that millimeter of space can save me in truth or make me again lose everything I have seen. It is perilous. Humankind praises highly what it senses. Which is as perilous as execrating what you sense.

I had offered God my Hell. And my cruelty, love of mine, my cruelty had suddenly stopped. And suddenly that very desert was the still-vague outline of what was called paradise. The moistness of a paradise. Not something else, but rather that very same desert. And I was surprised just as one is surprised by a light that comes out of nowhere.

Did I understand that what I had experienced, that nucleus of Hellish rapacity, was what is called love? But— neutral love?

Neutral love. The neutral was whispering. I was reaching what I had sought after for my whole life: something that is the most ultimate identity and that I had called inexpressive. It was that that had always been in my eyes in the pictures: an inexpressive happiness, a pleasure that does not know that it is pleasure—a pleasure too delicate for my coarse humanity that had always been made of coarse concepts.

"I had made so great an effort to talk to myself of a Hell without words. Now how can I speak of a love that contains only what is felt and before which the word "love" is just a dusty object?"

The Hell I have gone through—how can I explain it to you?—has been the Hell that comes from love. Oh, people attach the idea of sin to sex. But how innocent and infantile a sin that is. The real Hell is the Hell of love. Love is the experiencing of a greater danger in sin—it is the experiencing of the dirt and degradation and the worst of happiness. Sex is the startling of a child. But how can I speak to myself of the love that I now knew?

It's almost impossible. For in the neutrality of love there is a continuous happiness, like a rustling of leaves in the wind. And I fitted within the neutral nakedness of the woman on the wall. The same neutrality, the neutrality that had consumed me in pernicious, avid happiness, it was in that same neutrality that I was now hearing another kind of continuous happiness of love. What God is lay more in the neutral rustling of leaves in the wind than in my old human prayer.

Unless I could make my prayer true and it would seem to others and to me to be the cabala of a black magic, a neutral murmuring.

That murmuring without any human sense would be my identity touching the identity of things. I know that, in relation to the human, that neutral prayer would be a monstrosity. But in relation to him who is God, it would be: being.

I had been forced to go into the desert to find out with horror that the desert is alive, to find out that a cockroach is life. I had gone back until I found out that, in me, the most profound life is before human life—and to do that I had had the diabolical courage to let go of my feelings. I had had to avoid giving human value to life in order to understand the largeness, the much-more-than-human magnitude, of God. Had I asked for the most dangerous and forbidden of things? would I, risking my soul, have daringly demanded to see God?

And now it was as though I was before Him and did not understand—I was uselessly on my feet before Him, and it was once more a nothingness that I was before. For me, as for all of us, everything had been given, but I wanted more: I wanted to know about that everything. And I had sold my soul to know. But I now understood that I had not sold it to the devil but much more dangerously: to God. That He had let me see. For He knew that I wouldn't know how to see whatever I saw: the explanation of an enigma is the mere repetition of the enigma. What are You? and the answer is: You are. What do you exist? and the answer is: what you exist. I had the ability to question but not the ability to hear the answer.

No, I hadn't even been able to formulate the question. Nevertheless, the answer had continually posed itself to me since I was born. It had been because of that insistent answer that, in a reverse path, I had been forced to look for the question to which it corresponded. Then I had lost myself in a labyrinth of questions, and I asked questions at random, hoping that one of them might occasionally correspond to the question for my answer, and then I might be able to understand the answer.

But I was like a person who, having been born blind and having no sighted person at her side, that person couldn't even formulate a question about vision: she couldn't know that seeing existed. But, since vision did truly exist, even if that person didn't know it within herself and had never heard of it, that person would be still, anxious, alert, without being able to ask questions about what she didn't know existed . . . she would miss what should have been hers.

She would miss what should have been hers.

"No. I haven't told you all of it. I still wanted to see if I could escape relying on myself just a little. But my liberation will be realized only if I have the openness of my own lack of understanding."

Because, sitting there on the bed, I then said to myself:

"I have been given everything, and just look at what that everything is! it's a cockroach that is living and is close to death. And then I looked at the door latch. After that, I looked at the wood on the wardrobe. I looked at the window glass. Just look at what that all is: it's pieces of something, a piece of iron, of sand, of glass. I told myself: look what I have struggled for, to have exactly what I had before, I crawled until the doors opened for me, the doors of the treasure-room I was looking for: and look at what that treasure was!"

The treasure was a piece of metal, it was a piece of whitewash on a wall, it was a piece of matter made into a cockroach.

In prehistory I had begun my march through the desert, and without a star to guide me, only perdition guiding me, only error guiding me—until, almost dead from the ecstasy of fatigue, lighted by passion, I finally found the strongbox. And in the strongbox, the sparkle of glory, the hidden secret. The most remote secret in the world, opaque, but blinding me with the radiation of its simple existence, sparkling there in a glory that hurt my eyes. Inside the strongbox, the secret:

Pieces of something.

A piece of iron, a cockroach antenna, a chunk of mortar from the wall.

My exhaustion prostrated itself at the feet of the piece of something, in Hellish adoration. The secret of power was power, the secret of love was love—and the jewel of the world is an opaque piece of something.

The opacity reverberated in my eyes. The secret of my millenary trajectory of orgy and death and glory and thirst until I finally found what I always had, and for that I first had to die. Oh, I am being so direct that I am starting to seem symbolic.

A piece of something? the secret of the pharoahs. And because of that secret I had almost given my life . . .

More, much more: to have that secret that I still couldn't understand, I would again give my life. I had risked the world in search of the question that comes after the answer. An answer that remained a secret, even after what question it corresponded to had been revealed. I hadn't found a human answer to the enigma. But much more, oh much more: I had found the enigma itself. Too much had been given me. What could I do with what had been given me? "Let the holy thing not be given to dogs."

And I was not even touching the thing. I was just touching the space that goes from me to the vital core—I was within the cohesive, controlled area of the vital core's resonance. The vital core resonates at the resonance of my approach.

My closest possible approach stops a pace away. What keeps the step forward from being taken? It is the opaque irradiation simultaneously of the thing and of myself. We repel each other through similarity; through similarity we do not enter each other. And if the step were to be taken?

I don't know, I don't know. For the thing can never be really touched. The vital core is a finger pointing to it— and what is pointed to enlivens like a milligram of radium in the tranquil darkness. Then the wet crickets start to be heard. The milligram's light does not change the dark. For the dark is not lightable, the dark is a way of being: the dark is the dark's vital core, and something's vital core is never reached.

For me, will the thing have to be reduced to being just what surrounds the thing's untouchability? My God, give me what you have done. Or have you already given it to me? and am *I* the one who cannot take the step that will give me what you have done? Am I what you have done? and I can't take the step toward myself, me whom You are, Thing and Yourself. Give me what you are in me. Give me what you are in the others, You are the he, I know, I know because when I touch, I see the he. But the he, man, takes care of what you have given him and wraps himself in a husk made especially for me to touch and see. And I want more than the shell that I also love. I want what I love You.

But beyond the shell I had found only the enigma itself. And I trembled all over for fear of God.

I tremble with fear and adoration for what exists.

What exists and is just a piece of something, still I have to put my hand over my eyes against the opacity of that thing. Oh, the violent amorous unconsciousness of what exists surpasses the possibility of my consciousness. I am afraid of so much matter—matter resonates with attention, resonates with process, resonates with inherent nowness. What exists beats with strong waves against the unbreakable grain that is I, and that grain tumbles among the abysses of tranquil billows of existence, tumbles and does not dissolve, that seed-grain.

What am I the seed of? Seed of thing, seed of existence, seed of those very billows of neutral love. I, a person, am a germ. The germ is merely sensitive—that is its only particular quality. The germ suffers pain. The germ is eager and cunning. My eagerness is my most initial hunger: I am pure because I am eager.

Of the germ that I am, this happy matter, the thing, is also made. Which is an existence satisfied with its own process, profoundly occupied in just its own process, and the process resonates through all of it. That piece of thing inside the strongbox is the casket's secret. And the casket is itself made of the same secret, the strongbox in which the world's jewel is found, it too is made of the same secret.

Oh, and I don't want all of that! I hate what I have come to see. I don't want that world made of thing!

I don't want it. But I can't keep from feeling myself all filled out inside by the poverty of opacity and neutrality: the thing is alive like weeds. And if that is Hell, it is paradise itself: the choice is mine. It is I who shall be demonic or an angel; if I am demonic, this is Hell; if I am an angel, this is paradise. Oh, I shall send my angel on ahead to prepare the path before me. No, not my angel: but my humanity and its compassion.

I sent my angel on ahead to prepare the path before me and to tell the stones that I was coming so they could be softened for my lack of comprehension.

And it was my softest angel that found the piece of thing. It could find only what it was. For even when something falls from the sky it is a meteorite, that is, a piece of thing. My angel allows me to adore a piece of iron or glass.

But it is I who should keep myself from giving the things a name. A name is an accretion, and it inhibits contact with the thing. The name of the thing is an interval for the thing. The will to accretion is great . . . because bare things are so wearing.

Because bare things are so wearing.

Oh, then that was the reason I had always had a sort of love for tedium. And a continual hatred of it.

Because tedium is bland and so resembles the thing. And I had not been big enough: only big people love monotony. Contact with the supersound of the atonal has an inexpressive happiness about it that only the flesh tolerates, in love. Big people have the vital quality of the flesh, and they not only tolerate the atonal but aspire to it.

My old constructs had consisted in continually trying to transform the atonal into tone, in dividing the infinite into a series of finites, and in not comprehending that the finite is not a quantity, it is a quality. And my great discomfort in all of that had been feeling that, no matter how large the set of finites might be, it would not exhaust the residual quality of the infinite.

But tedium—tedium had been the only way I had been able to sense the atonal. And I hadn't known that I liked tedium only because I suffered from it. But in regard to living, suffering is not the measure of life: suffering is but a fateful subproduct, and, because it is sharper, it is negligible.

Oh, and I should have understood all that before! I who considered the inexpressive to be my secret concern. An inexpressive face fascinated me; the moment that was not climactic attracted me. Nature, what I liked in nature, was its vibrant inexpressiveness.

"Oh, I don't know how to explain it to you, since I am eloquent only when I err, error makes me deliberate and think. But how can I talk to you if there is a silence when I say the right thing? How can I tell you about the inexpressible?"

Even in tragedy, for real tragedy resides in the inexorability of its inexpressiveness, which is its bare identity.

At times—at times we manifest inexpressiveness ourselves—in art that is done, in bodily love too—to manifest the inexpressive is to create. At bottom we are so, so happy! for there is not just one way to enter into contact with life, there are also the negative ways! also the painful ways, even the all-but-impossible ones—and all that, all that before we die, all that even while we are awake! And there is also at times the exasperation of the atonal, which is a profound happiness: exasperated atonality is flight rising—nature is exasperated atonality, thus it was that worlds were formed: atonality became exasperated.

And let us look to the leaves, being heavy and green as they are, they have exasperated into things, for blind are the leaves and green they are. And let us feel in our hands how everything has weight, weight does not escape the inexpressive hand. Let the person who is completely absent not be awakened, whoever is absorbed is feeling the weight of things. One of the proofs of the thing is weight: only something with weight can fly. And the only thing that can fall—celestial meteorite—is something that has weight.

Or is all this just my still wanting the pleasure of the words for things? or is it my still wanting the orgasm of utmost beauty, of understanding, of the consummate act of love?

Because tedium is made of too primary a happiness! And that is why paradise is intolerable to me. I don't want paradise, I long to go back to Hell! I am not equal to the task of staying in paradise because paradise has no human taste! it has the taste of thing, and the vital thing had no taste, just like blood in my mouth when I cut myself and suck the blood, I am frightened because my own blood has no human taste.

And mother's milk, which is human, mother's milk is prehuman by far, and it has no taste, it is nothing, I have tried it—it is like the sculpted eye of a statue, which is empty and expressionless, for when art is good it is because it has touched inexpressiveness, the worst art is expressive art, the kind that transgresses the piece of iron and the piece of glass, and the smiles, and the shouts.

"Oh, hand that holds me, if I had not needed so much of myself to form my life, I would have had life!"

But on the human plane that would have been destruction: living life instead of living one's own life is forbidden. It is a sin to go into divine matter. And that sin has an inexorable punishment: the person who dares go into that secret, in losing her individual life, disorganizes the human world. I could also have left my solid construction in the air, even knowing that it was dismantleable . . . if it hadn't been for temptation. And temptation can keep one from getting to the other shore.

But why not stay inside, without trying to cross to the opposite bank? Staying inside the thing is madness. I don't want to stay inside, for if I do my prior humanization, which was so gradual, would come to have had no basis.

And I don't want to lose my humanity! oh, losing it

hurts, my sweet, like leaving a still-living body that refuses to die, like the cut-up pieces of a lizard.

But now it was too late. I would have to be bigger than my fear, and I would have to see what my prior humanization had been made of. Oh, I have to believe with such faith in the true, hidden seed of my humanity that I shouldn't be afraid of seeing humanization on the inside.

I shouldn't be afraid of seeing humanization on the inside.

"Give me your hand again, I still don't know how to console myself about truth."

But—sit here a moment with me—the greatest disbelief in the truth of humanization would be to think that truth would destroy humanization. Wait for me, wait: I know that later on I'll learn how to fit all that into daily practice—don't forget that I too need daily life!

But look, love of mine, truth can't be bad. The truth is what it is—and precisely because it is immutably what it is, it had to be our great security, just as desiring our father or our mother is so inevitable that it has to have been our basis. That is it, then, the way, do you understand? why should I be afraid of consuming good or evil? if they exist it is because that is what exists.

Wait for me, I know that I am moving toward something that hurts because I am losing other things—but wait for me to go on a little farther. From all this, who knows, a name may be born! a name without word, but one that will perhaps set the roots of truth in my human formation.

Don't be afraid like I am afraid: it can't be bad to

have seen life in its very plasma. It is dangerous, it is sinful, but it can't be bad, because we are made of that plasma.

"Listen, don't be afraid: remember that I have eaten the forbidden fruit and was nonetheless not struck down by the orgy of being. Listen, then: that means that I shall save myself even more than I would have saved myself if I hadn't eaten of life. . . . Listen, it is because I dove into the abyss that I am beginning to love the abyss I am made of. Identity can be dangerous because of the intense pleasure that may become mere pleasure and nothing more. But I am now accepting love for the thing."

It isn't dangerous, I swear it isn't dangerous.

For the state of grace exists permanently: we are always saved. The whole world is in a state of grace. A person is smitten by sweetness only when she perceives that she is in the state of grace, to sense when you are in grace is itself the gift, and few take the risk of recognizing that in themselves. But there is no danger of perdition, I know that now: the state of grace is inherent.

"Listen. I was accustomed only to transcending. Hope, for me, had been deferral. I had never left my soul free, and I had quickly organized myself into a person because it is too risky to lose form. But now I see what was really happening to me. I had so little faith that I had merely invented the future, I believed so little in what exists that I had deferred nowness for a promise and for a future."

But now I discover that it isn't even necessary to have hope.

It is much more serious. Oh, I know that I am getting involved again in dangerous matters and that I ought to leave off speaking to myself. One shouldn't say that hope isn't necessary, for that could end up being changed, since

I am weak, into a destructive weapon. And for you, it could end up being changed into a useful weapon of destruction.

I might not understand and you might not understand that doing away with hope . . . in fact implies action, and right now. No, it isn't destructive—wait, let me understand us. It's a forbidden topic not because there's anything bad about it but because we put ourselves at risk.

I know that for me to abandon what was a life completely organized by hope, I know that abandoning all that—in favor of that wider something that is just being alive—abandoning all that hurts like separating from a yet-unborn child. Hope is a yet-unborn, only promised child, and that is crushing.

But I know that at one and the same time I want and don't want to hold myself back anymore. It's like being in a death agony: within death something wants to get free and simultaneously is afraid to leave the safety of the body. I know that it is perilous to speak about lack of hope, but listen—there is a profound alchemy taking place inside of me, and it was forged in the fire of Hell. And that gives me the greater right: the right to err.

Listen without fright or suffering: God's neutrality is so great and vital that I, because I could not bear God's cell, I had humanized it. I know that it is horribly dangerous to discover now that God has the power of impersonality . . . because I know, oh, I know! that it is as if that meant the destruction of entreaty!

It is as if the future stopped emerging. And we can do nothing about it, we are deficient.

But listen a minute: I'm not speaking of the future, I'm speaking of a permanent nowness. And that means that hope doesn't exist because it is no longer a deferred future, it is now. Because God doesn't promise. He is much greater than that: He is and never ceases being. It is we who cannot bear this ever-now light, and so we promise it for later only so we do not have to feel it right now, today. The present is God's today face. The horror is that we know that it is right in life that we see God. It is with our eyes truly open that we see God. And if I put the face of reality off until after my death—it is through guile, for I prefer to be dead at the time of seeing Him, and so I think I won't really see Him, just as I have courage really to dream only when I am sleeping.

I know that what I am feeling is serious and has the power to destroy me. Because—because it is as though I were telling myself that the kingdom of heaven is now.

And I don't want the kingdom of heaven, I don't want it, I can bear only its promise! The message I am getting from myself sounds cataclysmic to me, and once again close to the diabolical. But that is only for fear. It is fear. For doing away with hope means that I have to begin to live and not just to promise myself that I will. And that is the greatest fright I can have. Before, I waited. But God is now: His kingdom has just begun.

And His kingdom, my precious, is also of this world. I didn't have the courage to stop being a promise, and I promised myself, like an adult who doesn't have the courage to see that she has become an adult and keeps promising herself maturity.

And that's how I knew that the divine promise of life is now being fulfilled, and that it has always been fulfilled. Previously, only from time to time was I reminded, in a vision instantaneous and then suddenly remote, that promise is not only for the future, it is yesterday and it is permanently today: but that was jarring for me. I preferred to keep on entreating, without having the courage to have, now.

And I do have. I shall always have. It's only needing that I have. Needing never stops, for needing is the nature of my neutrality. What I do with entreaty and with lacking . . . that will be the life I shall have made of my life. Not putting myself in the face of hope isn't the destruction of entreaty! and it isn't abstention from lack. Oh, it is rather to add to it, it is to add infinitely to the entreaty born of lack.

To add infinitely to the entreaty born of lack.

It isn't for us that cows' milk comes forth, but we drink it. Flowers weren't made for us to look at or for us to smell, and we look at them and smell them. The Milky Way doesn't exist for us to know of its existence, but we know. And we know God. And what we need of Him, we get out of that. (I don't know what it is I'm calling God, but it can be called that.) If we know but very little about God, it is because we need little: we have of Him only what is destined to sustain us, we have of God what fits in us. (Nostalgia is not for the God who is missing to us, it is a nostalgia for ourselves, for we do not sustain ourselves; we miss our impossible grandeur—my unreachable nowness is my paradise lost.)

We suffer because we have so little hunger, although our small hunger is still enough for us to feel the profound loss of the pleasure we would have if we had a greater hunger. Milk people drink only as much as the body needs, and flowers we see only as far as the eyes reach and their fullness skims. However much more we need, the more God exists. However much farther we reach, that much more of God shall we have.

He enables us. (He wasn't born for us, nor were we born for Him, we and He are, at the same time.) He is uninterruptedly occupied in being, like all things are being, but He doesn't keep people from joining Him and, with Him, being occupied in being, in an interchange as fluid and constant . . . as the interchange of living. He, for example, He uses us totally, for there is nothing in each one of us that He, whose need is absolutely infinite, doesn't need. He uses us, and doesn't keep people from making use of Him. The ore in the earth isn't responsible for not being used.

We are very far behind and have no idea of how to take advantage of God in an interchange—as though we still hadn't discovered that milk is for drinking. A few centuries ago, or a few minutes ago we may perhaps say, in alarm: and to think that God was always there! the one who was there very little was I—just as we would say of oil that people finally needed enough to learn how to extract it from the earth, just as one day we will lament those who have died of cancer without using the cure that is at hand. Surely we still don't need to die of cancer. Everything is at hand. (Perhaps beings on another planet already know these things and already live in an interchange that is natural for them; for us, now, that interchange would amount to "holiness" and would completely confound our lives.)

Cows' milk we drink. And if the cow doesn't let us, we have recourse to violence. (In life and in death anything goes, living is always a life-and-death question.) With God too you can make your way through violence. He Himself, when he especially needs one of us, He chooses us and violates us.

But my violence toward God has to be a violence toward myself. I have to do violence to myself so I can need more. So that I become so desperately greater that I become empty and needy. I shall thus have touched the root of needing. The great emptiness in me will be where I exist; my extreme poverty will be a great will. I have to do violence to myself until I have nothing and need everything; when I need then I will have, for I know that it is only just to give more to the one who asks for more, my demand is my size, my emptiness my measure. You can also do violence directly unto God, with a love full of anger.

And He will understand that that furious, murderous avidity of ours is in fact our sacred, vital fury, our attempt to violate ourselves, the effort to eat more than we can so as to increase our hunger artificially—in the demand for life everything is legitimate, even the artificial, and the artificial is often the great sacrifice that is made to get to the essential.

But, since we are little and therefore need but little, why is little not enough for us? Because we sense pleasure. Like blind men who feel their way along, we have presentiments of the intense pleasure of living.

And if we have presentiments, it is also because we feel that we are being alarmingly used by God, we feel alarmingly that we are being used with an intense and uninterrupted pleasure—moreover, up to now our salvation has been one of being at least so used, we are not useless, we have been made intense use of by God; body and soul and life are for that: for someone's interchange and ecstasy. Disquieted, we feel that we are being used every minute—but that awakens in us the disquieting desire to use as well.

And He not only allows but needs to be used, being used is a way of being understood. (In all religions God demands to be loved.) For us to have, all we need is to need. To need is always the supreme moment. Just as the most daring happiness between a man and a woman comes when needing becomes so great that it is felt in agony and wonder: without you I will be unable to live. Love's revelation is a revelation of lacking—blessed be the poor of spirit for the sundering realm of life is theirs.

If I abandon hope, I am celebrating my lack, and that is the greatest solemnity of living. And because I have taken up my lack, life is at hand. Many have been those who have abandoned everything they had and set out in search of a greater hunger.

Oh, I have lost timidity: God now is. We have already been proclaimed, and it has been my own errant life that has proclaimed me to the right one. Beatitude is the continuous pleasure of the thing, the process of the thing is made of pleasure and of contact with what is gradually needed more and more. My whole fraudulent struggle came from my not wanting to assume the promise that can be fulfilled: I didn't want reality.

For to be real is to take up the promise itself: to assume innocence itself and take up again the taste we were never aware of: the taste of the living.

The taste of the living.

Which is an almost nonexistent taste. And that because things are very delicate. Oh, the efforts to experience the Host.

The thing is so delicate it astonishes me that it ever becomes visible. And there are things so much more delicate that they are not visible. But they all have a delicacy equivalent to what it means for our body to have a face: that sensitization of the body that is a human face. The thing has a sensitization about itself that is like a face.

Oh, and I didn't know how to consubstantiate my "soul." It isn't immaterial, it is of the most delicate thing-material. It is thing, but what I can't do is consubstantiate it in visible depth.

Oh, my love, things are very delicate. People tread upon them with too many human feet, with too many sentiments. Only the delicacy of innocence or only the delicacy of the initiate senses its almost nonexistent taste. Before, I needed seasoning for everything, and in that way I skipped over the thing and tasted the taste of the seasoning.

I couldn't taste the taste of a potato, because a potato is almost earth matter; the potato is so delicate that—

because of my inability to live on the delicacy level of the merely earthly taste of a potato—I put my human foot on top of it and broke its living-thing delicacy. Because living matter is very innocent.

And my own innocence? I ache of it. Because I also know that, on the merely human plane, innocence is having the cruelty that the cockroach has with itself in slowly dying without pain; to transcend pain is the highest cruelty. And I am afraid of that, I who am extremely moral. But I now know that I have to have a much greater courage: the courage to have another morality, so empty that I don't understand it myself and it frightens me.

"Oh, I haven't forgotten you who are the oldest thing in my memory. I see you again, putting the wires together to fix the electric plug, being careful of the positive and negative lines, and handling things delicately."

I didn't know that I had learned so much from you. What did I learn? I learned to look at a person putting together electric wires. I learned to see you fix a broken chair once. Your physical energy was your most delicate energy.

"You were the oldest person I had ever met. You were the monotony of my eternal love, and I didn't know it. I had for you the same tedium that I feel on holidays. What was it like? it was like water running in a stone fountain, and the years marked on its smooth stone, the moss half-pushed back by the current of running water, and the cloud above, and the beloved man in repose, and static love, it was a holiday, and the silence in the mosquitoes' flight. And the available present. And my slightly boring liberty, the fullness, the fullness of a body that does not seek and does not need."

I didn't know how to see that that was a delicate love. And it seemed like tedium to me. It was in fact tedium. It was a person's quest to frolic, the wish to plumb the depths of the air, to contact the air in the profoundest way, the air that is not there to be plumbed, that is destined to remain suspended as it is.

I don't know, I remember that it was a holiday. Oh how much I wanted pain then: it would distract me from that great divine emptiness that I had with you. I, the goddess in repose; you, on Olympus. The great yawn of happiness? Distance following itself distantly, and the other distance, and yet another—the fullness of space that a holiday has. That unfolding of calm energy, I didn't even understand. That now-thirstless kiss on the distracted forehead of the beloved man in repose, the pensive kiss of the man now loved. It was a national holiday. Flags hoisted.

But night falling. And I couldn't bear the slow transformation of something that is slowly transforming itself into the same something, merely added to by yet another identical drop of time. I recall that I told you:

"I have a little bit of a stomachache," I said, breathing with some satiety. "What shall we do tonight?"

"Nothing," you answered, so much wiser than I. "Nothing, it's a holiday," said the man who was delicate with things and with time.

The profound tedium—like a great love—bound us together. And the next morning, early in the morning, the world was opening itself to me. Things' wings were open, it was going to be a hot afternoon, you could feel it in the cool sweat of the things that had passed the tepid night, like in a hospital where the patients awake still alive.

But all that was too fine for my human foot. And I, I sought beauty.

But now I have a morality that dispenses with beauty. I shall have to bid a nostalgic good-bye to beauty. Beauty was a soft enticement to me, it was the way I, weak and respectful, adorned the thing to be able to bear its core.

But now my world is the world of the thing that before I would have called ugly or monotonous — and is neither ugly nor monstrous to me anymore. I have gone through gnawing the earth, through eating the ground, and I have gone through having that kind of an orgy, and through feeling with moral horror that the earth I gnawed also felt pleasure. My orgy in fact came from my puritanism: pleasure offended me, and from the offense I created greater pleasure. Nevertheless, this present world of mine, I would have called it violent before.

For water's tastelessness is violent, the colorlessness of a piece of glass is violent. A violence is all the more violent because it is neutral.

My present world is raw, it is a world of a great vital difficulty. For, more than a star, I now wish the thick, black root of the stars, I wish the source that always seems dirty, and is dirty, and is always incomprehensible.

It is with pain that I bid good-bye to the beauty of a child — I want the adult, who is more primitive and ugly and drier and more difficult, and who has become a seed-child that can't be broken between the teeth.

Oh, and I want to see too if I can now dispense with horses drinking water, which are so pretty. I also do not want my sensibility because it makes beauty; and could I dispense with the sky moving in clouds? and with flowers? I don't want pretty love. I don't want half-light, I don't want a well-made face, I don't want the expressive. I want the inexpressive. I want the inhuman within the person; no, it isn't dangerous, for a person is human anyway, it isn't necessary to struggle for that: wanting to be human sounds too pretty to me.

I want the materiality of things. Humanity is steeped in humanization, as though it were necessary; and that false humanization impedes man and impedes his humanity. There exists a thing that is broader, deafer, and deeper, less good, less bad, less pretty. Even though that thing too runs the risk of becoming transformed into "purity" in our gross hands, our hands that are gross and full of words.

Our hands that are gross and full of words.

"You'll have to bear my telling you that God isn't pretty. I say that because He is neither a result nor a conclusion, and everything that people find pretty is often only because it is already brought to a close. But what is ugly today will be seen as beauty centuries from now, because it will have completed one of its movements."

I don't want any longer the completed movement that in reality is never completed but that we complete in our desire; I don't want any longer to enjoy the ease of liking something simply because, since it is apparently complete, it no longer frightens me, and then is falsely mine—I, devourer of beauty that I was.

I don't want beauty, I want identity. Beauty would be an accretion, and I am going to dispense with it. The world has no intention of beauty, and that would have shocked me before: in the world there exists no aesthetic plane, not even the aesthetic plane of goodness, and that would have shocked me before. The thing is much more than that. God is greater than goodness and its beauty.

Oh, getting rid of all that means so great a disillusionment. But it is in disillusionment that the promise is fulfilled, through disillusionment, through pain that the promise is fulfilled, and it is for that reason that one must first pass through Hell: until one sees that there is a much deeper way of loving and that way does away with the accretion of beauty. God is what exists, and all the contradictions are within God, and therefore they don't contradict Him.

Oh, everything in me is aching to leave what was the world for me. Leaving is so harsh and aggressive an attitude that a person who opens her mouth to talk of leaving should be arrested and held incommunicado — I prefer to consider myself temporarily out of my own control rather than have the courage to think that all that is true.

"Give me your hand, don't leave me, I swear that I too didn't want it: I too lived well, I was a woman to whom you could refer with the phrase 'the life and loves of G. H.' I can't put the system into words, but I lived in a system. It was as though I organized myself around the fact of having a stomachache because, if I no longer had it, I would also lose the marvelous hope of one day getting rid of the stomachache: my old life was necessary to me because it was precisely its error that made me take up imagining a hope that, without the life that I led, I wouldn't have known."

And now I am risking an entire entrenched hope, in favor of a reality so much greater that I cover my eyes with my arm because I can't face head-on a hope so immediately fulfillable — even before I die! So much before I die. I also scorch myself in that discovery: the discovery that there exists a morality in which beauty is a huge, timid superficiality. Now what invokes me and calls me is neutrality. I have no words to express it, and I therefore speak of neutrality. I have only that ecstasy that too is no longer what we have been calling ecstasy, for it isn't culmination. But that culminationless ecstasy expresses the neutrality of which I speak.

Oh, to speak to myself and to you is being mute. To speak to God is what exists that is even more mute. To speak to things is mute. I know that that sounds sad to you, and to me as well, for I am still corrupted by the condiment of the word. And that is the reason that silence hurts me like an abandonment.

But I know that I must abandon myself: contact with the thing must be a murmur, and to speak to God I must put together unconnected syllables. My lacking came from the fact that I had lost my inhuman side — I had been expelled from paradise when I became human. And true prayer is the silent oratorio of inhumanity.

No, I don't have to rise through prayer: I must, ingurgitated, make myself a resonant nothingness. What I speak to God about has to make no sense! If it makes sense, it is because I err.

Oh, don't misunderstand me: I am taking nothing away from you. What I am doing is demanding of you. I know that it seems like I am taking away your and my humanity. But it's exactly the opposite: what I want is to live of that initial and primordial something that was what made some things reach the point of aspiring to be human. What I want for myself is to live of the most difficult part of humanity: to live of the germ of neutral love, for it was from that source that there began to sprout what later became distorted into sentimentations to the extent that the core became suffocated by the accretion of richness and squashed inside us by the human foot. It is a much greater love that I am demanding of myself — it is so much greater a life that it doesn't even contain beauty.

I now have that hard courage that hurts me like the flesh transformed in childbirth.

But no, I still haven't told all.

Not that what I'm going to tell now is all that's left. Much more has been left out of this account that I am giving to myself; father and mother are missing, for example; I still haven't had the courage to honor them; many of the humiliations I have gone through are missing, and I omit them because the only people who are humiliated are those who aren't humble, and instead of humiliation I should talk about my lack of humility; and humility is much more than a feeling, it is reality seen through minimal good sense.

Much yet remains to tell. But there is one thing that it will be imperative to say.

(One thing I know: if I reach the end of this account, I'll go, not tomorrow but yet today, to eat and dance at the Top-Bambino, I mightily need to have a good time and distract myself. I'll be sure to wear my new blue dress that makes me look a little thinner and gives me color, I'll phone Carlos, Josefina, Antonio, I don't remember clearly which one of the two men I thought might be in love with me or if both were, I'll eat *crevettes* and not worry about how many, and I know why I'll eat *crevettes* tonight, tonight my regular life will be starting again, the life of my common happiness, I'll need for the rest of my days my slight, sweet, good-humored commonness, I, like everybody, need to forget.)

But I haven't told everything.

But I haven't told everything.

I haven't said how, sitting there motionless, I still hadn't stopped looking with deep disgust, yes, still with disgust, at the yellowed white mass on top of the cockroach's grayness. And I knew that as long as I had that disgust the world would evade me and I would evade myself. I knew that the basic error in living was finding cockroaches disgusting. Finding disgust in the thought of kissing a leper was my missing the primary life inside me . . . for disgust contradicts me, contradicts my matter in me.

Then what, in pity for myself, I didn't want to think, then, I thought. I couldn't hold myself back anymore, and I thought that I was now truly thinking.

Now, in pity of the anonymous hand that I hold in mine, in pity for what that hand is not going to comprehend, I don't wish to take it with me to the horror that yesterday I went to alone.

For I suddenly knew not only that the moment had arrived to understand I could no longer transcend but also that the instant had arrived when I really could no longer transcend. And to have now what I always before thought should be for tomorrow. I am trying to save you, but I cannot.

For redemption must be in the thing itself. And redemption in the thing itself would be my putting into my own mouth the white paste from the cockroach.

At just the idea I closed my eyes with the force of someone locking her jaws, and I clenched my teeth so tight that any more and they would break right inside my mouth. My insides said no, my mass rejected the cockroach's mass.

I had stopped sweating; I had dried completely out again. I tried to reason with my disgust. Why should I be disgusted by the mass that came out of the cockroach? had I not drunk of the white milk that is the liquid maternal mass? and when I drank the stuff that my mother was made of, hadn't I, wordlessly, called it love? But reason didn't get me anywhere, except to keep my teeth clenched together as though they were made of flesh that was ashiver.

I couldn't.

There was only one way I could: if I gave myself a hypnotic command, and then I could in effect go to sleep and act as though I were in a sleepwalking trance—and when I opened my eyes from that sleep the thing would be "done," and it would be like a bad dream you wake up feeling free from because you were dreaming that your life was so much worse.

But I knew that I couldn't do it that way. I knew that I would really have to eat the cockroach mass, and all of me eat it, even my very fear eat it. Only then would I have what suddenly seemed to me to be the anti-sin: to eat the cockroach mass is the anti-sin, sin that would kill myself.

The anti-sin. But at what a price.

At the price of my going through the sensation of death.

I arose and took a step forward, with the determination not of someone who is bent on suicide but of someone who is going to kill herself.

The sweat had begun again, I was now dripping from head to toe, the honeyed toes of my feet ran inside my slippers, and the roots of my hair softened before that viscous thing that was my new sweat, a sweat that I didn't recognize and that had a smell like the smell that comes up from parched ground when it gets the first rain. That profound sweat was, however, what gave me life, I was slowly swimming in the oldest broth of my culture, the sweat was plankton and pneuma and *pabulum vitae*, I was being, I was being me.

No, my darling, it wasn't good in the sense that we use the word good. It was what we call awful. In fact, very, very awful. For the root of me, that I was only now experiencing, had the taste of a potato tuber, mixed with the earth it had been pulled out of. Nevertheless, that bad taste had a strange grace of living that I can understand only if I sense it again and can explain only while I do.

I took another step forward. But instead of going on ahead, I suddenly threw up the bread and the milk I had eaten at breakfast that morning.

Shaken through and through by the violent vomiting, which had come without any warning nausea, disappointed with myself, frightened by my lack of strength to carry out an act that seemed to me to be the only thing that would bring my soul and body together again.

Despite myself, after vomiting I had become serene, my head relieved, physically calm.

What was worse: I still had to eat the cockroach, but without the aid of my prior exaltation, the exaltation that would have acted within me like hypnosis; I had thrown up my exaltation. And unexpectedly, after the revolution that is vomiting, I felt physically simple like a child. It would have to be in that state, like a child carelessly happy, that I would eat the cockroach mass.

Then I stepped forward.

My happiness and my shame came when I awoke from my faint. No, it hadn't been a faint. It had been more like a dizzy spell, for I was still on my feet, my hand propped against the wardrobe. A dizzy spell that had made me lose track of the moments, of time. But I knew, even before thinking, that, while I had been gone in the dizzy spell, "something had happened."

I didn't want to think about it, but I knew. I was afraid to taste in my mouth what I was tasting, I was afraid to run my hand over my lips and feel any remains. I was afraid to look toward the cockroach—which must now have less of a white mass on its opaque back . . .

I was ashamed that I had had to become dizzy and unconscious to do something that now I would never afterward know how I did . . . for I had taken away all my participation before I did it. I hadn't really wanted to "know."

Was that, then, the way we do things? "Not knowing"—was that the way the most profound things happened? would something always, always have to be apparently dead for the really living to happen? had I had not to know that it was living? Was the secret of never escaping from the greater life the secret of living like a sleepwalker?

Or was living like a sleepwalker the greatest act of confidence? the act of closing your eyes in dizziness and never knowing what took place.

Like a transcendence. Transcendence, which is the remembrance of the past or of the present or of the future. In me was transcendence the only way I could reach the thing? For even in eating of the cockroach, I had acted by transcending the very act of eating. And now all I was left with was the vague recollection of a horror, I was left with only the idea.

Until the recollection was so strong that my body shouted all in itself.

I dug my fingernails into the wall: now I tasted the bad taste in my mouth, and then I began to spit, to spit out furiously that taste of nothing at all, taste of a nothingness that nonetheless seemed to me almost sweetened with the taste of certain flower petals, taste of myself—I spit myself out, never reaching the point of feeling that I had finally spit out my whole soul. "Because you are neither hot nor cold, because you are tepid, I will vomit you out from my mouth," was the Revelation according to St. John, and the phrase, which must refer to other things that I now no longer remembered, the phrase came to me from the depths of my memory, serving as the insipidity of which I had eaten— and I was spitting.

Which was difficult: because the neutral thing is extremely energetic, I spat and spat and it kept on being me.

I only stopped in my fury when I realized with surprise that I was undoing everything I had laboriously done, when I realized that I was betraying myself. And that, poor me, I couldn't get beyond my own life.

I stopped, shocked, and my eyes filled with tears that just burned and didn't run. I think I didn't feel that I was even worthy of having tears run, I lacked the basic pity for myself that lets one cry, and I retained in my burning pupils the tears that spread salt on me and that I didn't deserve to have run.

But even though they didn't run, the tears were such companions to me and bathed me with such compassion that I lowered a head that had been consoled. And, like one who returns from a trip, I sat down again quietly on the bed.

I who had thought that the best proof of my internal metamorphosis would be to put the cockroach's white mass into my mouth. And that in that way I would approach . . . the divine? the real? For me the divine is the real.

For me the divine is the real.

But kissing a leper isn't even goodness. It is reality in itself, it is life in itself—even if that also means the leper's salvation. But it is first one's own salvation. The saint's greatest benefit is to himself, which is unimportant: for when he reaches the great vastness itself, thousands of people are enlarged by his vastness and live on it, and he loves others just as much as he loves his own terrible vastness, he loves his opening-out with lack of pity for himself. Does the saint wish to purify himself because he feels the need to love the neutral? to love what is not an accretion, and to dispense with the good and the attractive. The saint's great goodness . . . is that for him everything is the same. The saint scorches himself until he reaches love of the neutral. He needs it for himself.

I then understood that, no matter the situation, living is a great good in relation to others. All one has to do is live, and that in itself brings about that great good. He who lives totally is living for others, he who lives his own vastness is giving a gift, even if his life takes place in the cloister of a cell. Living is so great a gift that thousands of people benefit from every lived day.

"Does it pain you that God's goodness is neutrally continuous and continuously neutral? But what I had wanted as a miracle, what I called "miracle," was in fact a desire for discontinuity and interruption, the desire for anomaly: what I called "miracle" was the precise moment when the true, continuous miracle of process was interrupted. But God's neutral goodness is still more entreatable than it would be if it weren't neutral: it is just going and having, just asking and having."

And miracles too can be sought and had, for continuity has interstices that don't make it discontinuous, the miracle is the note that lies between two musical notes, the number that lies between the number one and the number two. It's just a question of seeking and having. Faith . . . is knowing that you can go consume the miracle. Hunger, that is what faith is in and of itself—and needing is my guarantee that it will always be given to me. Necessity is my guide.

No. I didn't need to have the courage to eat the cockroach mass. For I lacked the saint's humility: I had given the act of eating it a sense of "maximum." But life is divided into qualities and species, and the law is that cockroaches will be loved and eaten only by other cockroaches; and that a woman, at the moment of her love for a man, that woman is experiencing her own species. I realized that I had just done the equivalent of experiencing the cockroach mass . . . for the law is that I should live with person-matter and not cockroach-matter.

I realized that by putting the cockroach mass in my mouth, I was not bereaving myself as saints bereave themselves, but rather I was again seeking accretion. Accretion is easier to love.

And now I am taking your hand in to my own. I am the one who is giving you my hand.

I need your hand now, not so I won't be afraid but so you won't. I know belief in all this will, in the beginning, be a great solitude for you. But the moment will arrive when you will give me your hand, no longer in solitude, but as I do now: in love. Just like me, you won't be afraid to add yourself to God's extreme energetic sweetness. Solitude is simply having human destiny.

And solitude is not needing. Not needing leaves a person alone, all alone. Oh, needing doesn't isolate a person, things need things: it's enough to see a chick walking to see that its destiny will be what lack will make of it, its destiny is to join, like drops of mercury cling to other drops of mercury, even though, like all drops of mercury, it has a complete and rounded existence in itself.

Oh, my love, don't be afraid of that lacking: it is our greater destiny. Love is so much more fateful than I thought, love is as ingrained as is lack itself, and we are guaranteed by necessity that it is continually renewed. Love is now, is always. All that is missing is the coup-de-grâce— which is called passion.

All that is missing is the coup-de-grâce—which is called passion.

What I am now feeling is a happiness. Through the live cockroach I am coming to understand that I too am that which lives. To live is a very high stage, it is something I have just now attained. It is so high an unstable equilibrium that I know I won't be able to stay aware of it for long—the grace of passion is short.

Perhaps to be human like us is merely a special sensitization that we call "having humanity." Oh, I also fear losing this sensitization. Till now I had called my sensitivity to life "life" itself. But to live is something else.

To live is a gross, radiating indifference. To be alive is unreachable by the most delicate of sensibilities. To be alive is inhuman—the deepest meditation is one that is so empty that a smile is exhaled as though it came from some matter. And I shall be even more delicate, and more permanent in my state. Am I speaking of death? am I speaking of after death? I don't know. I sense that "nonhuman" is a great reality, and that that doesn't mean "inhuman": to the contrary, the nonhuman is the radiating center of a neutral love in radio waves.

If my life is transformed into it-itself, what I now call sensibility will not exist—it will be called indifference. But I am still unable to learn that way of being. It is as if hundreds of thousands of years from now we finally won't be what we feel and think anymore: we shall have something that more closely resembles an "attitude" than an idea. We shall be living matter manifesting itself directly, unmindful of words, going beyond always-grotesque thinking.

And I won't travel "from thought to thought" but from attitude to attitude. We shall be inhuman—as humankind's greatest conquest. To be is to be beyond the human. To be a human being doesn't do it, to be human has been a constraint. The unknown awaits us, but I sense that that unknown is a totalization and will be the true humanization we long for. Am I speaking of death? no, of life. It isn't a state of felicity, it is a state of contact.

Oh, don't think that all this doesn't make me sick, in fact I find it so boring that it makes me impatient. But it resembles paradise, where I can't even imagine what I'd do, for I can only imagine myself thinking and feeling, two attributes of one's being, and I can't imagine myself just being and ignoring the rest. Just to be—that would leave me with an enormous need of something to do.

At the same time, I was a little bit doubtful.

The fact is that, just as earlier I had become terrified before by my entrance into what could develop into despair, I now suspected that I was again transcending things . . .

Could I be enlarging the thing too much precisely to go beyond the cockroach and the piece of iron and the piece of glass?

I don't think so.

For I wasn't reducing hope to a simple result of construction and counterfeiting, nor was I denying the existence of something to hope for. Nor was I removing the promise: I was merely sensing, with enormous effort, that hope and promise are fulfilled at every instant. And that was terrifying, I have always feared being stricken by realization, I had always thought of realization as a final resting point—and I hadn't foreseen a situation where necessity is ever being born.

And also since I was afraid, because I couldn't stand simple glory, that I would make it one more accretion. But I know—I know—that there is an experiencing of glory in which life has the purest taste of nothingness and that in glory I feel it to be empty. When living is realized, the question will be asked: but was that all there was to it? And the answer: that isn't *all* there is, it is exactly *what* there is to it.

Only I still have to be careful not to make more of it than that, for if I do it won't be that anymore. Essence is a piercing insipidity. I'll have to "purify myself" much more just not to want the accretion of events. Before, self-purification implied cruelty for me, against what I called beauty and against what I called "me," without knowing that "me" was an accretion to myself.

But now, through my most difficult fright I am finally moving toward the opposite path. I am moving toward the destruction of what I have constructed, I am moving toward depersonalization.

I am anxious for the world, I have strong, definite desires, tonight I'll go dancing and eating, I won't wear my blue dress, I'll wear my black-and-white one instead. But at the same time, I don't need anything. I don't even need a tree to exist. I now know a modality that dispenses with everything—and also with love, with nature, with objects. A mode that dispenses with me. Even though, as regards my desires, my passions, my contact with a tree—they may keep on being for me like a mouth eating.

Depersonalization like the deposing of useless individuality—the loss of everything that can be lost, while still being. To take away from yourself little by little, with an effort so attentive that no pain is felt, to take away from yourself like one who gets free of her own skin, her own characteristics. Everything that characterizes me is just the way I am most easily viewed by others and end up being superficially recognizable to myself. Just as there was the moment when I saw that the cockroach was the cockroach of all cockroaches, so too I want from me to encounter the woman of all women in myself.

Depersonalization as the great objectification of oneself. The greatest externalization one can attain. Whoever is touched by depersonalization will recognize the other in any guise: the first step in relation to the other is to find in oneself the man of all men. Every woman is the woman of all women, every man is the man of all men, and every one of them could appear wherever humankind is judged. But only in immanence, because only a few people reach the point of recognizing themselves in us. And then, in the simple presence of their existence, revealing our own.

What is lived of—and since it has no name only silence enunciates it—is what I approach through the great amplitude of ceasing to be myself. Not because I may then discover the name and make the impalpable concrete—but because I determine the impalpable to be impalpable, and then the breath builds again like in the flame of a candle.

The gradual deheroization of oneself is the true labor that is performed under merely apparent labor, life is a secret mission. Real life is so secret that not even I, who am dying of it, have been given the password, I am dying without knowing of what. And the secret is such that only if the mission is finally carried out do I, all of a sudden, see that I was born entrusted with it—all of life is a secret mission.

The deheroization of myself is undermining the ground beneath my edifice, doing so despite me like an unknown calling. Until it is finally revealed to me that life in me does not bear my name.

And I also have no name, and that is my name. And because I depersonalize to the point of not having a name, I shall answer every time someone says: me.

Deheroization is the grand failure of a life. Not everyone can fail because it is such hard work, one must first climb painfully up to get to the height to fall from—I can only achieve the depersonality of silence if I have first built an entire voice. My cultures were necessary to me so that I could climb up to have a point to come down from. It is precisely through the foundering of the voice that one hears for the first time one's own silence and that of others and of things, and accepts it as the possible language. Only then is my nature accepted, accepted with its wonderous torture in which pain isn't something that happens to us but what we are. And our condition is accepted as the only one possible since it is what exists and none other. And since the experience of it is our passion. The human condition is Christ's passion.

Oh, but to reach silence, what a huge effort of voice. My voice is the way I go to seek reality; reality prior to my language exists as an unthinkable thought, but I was and am fatefully impelled to have to know what thought thinks. Reality precedes the voice that seeks it, but like the earth precedes the tree, but like the world precedes the man, but like the sea precedes the view of the sea, life precedes love, bodily matter precedes the body, and one day in its turn language shall have preceded possession of silence.

I have to the extent that I determine—and that is the splendor of having a language. But I have much more to the extent that I am unable to determine. Reality is raw material, language the way I seek it—and how I don't find it. But it is from seeking and not finding that what I have not known is born, and I instantly recognize it. Language is my human endeavor. I have fatefully to go seeking and fatefully I return with empty hands. But—I return with the unsayable. The unsayable can be given me only through the failure of my language. Only when the construct falters do I reach what it could not accomplish.

And it is useless to try to take a shortcut and start right in, knowing already that the voice says little, starting already with depersonalization. For the trajectory exists, and the trajectory is more than just a way of proceeding. We ourselves *are* the trajectory. In living one can never arrive ahead of time. The *via crucis* isn't a wrong way, it is the only way, you get there only through it and with it. Insistence is our effort, desistance is the prize. One gets the prize when she has experienced the power of building and, in spite of the taste of power, prefers desistance. Desistance has to be a choice. To desist is a life's most sacred choice. To desist is the true human moment. And it alone is the glory proper to my condition.

Desistance is a revelation.

Desistance is a revelation.

I desist, and I shall have been the human person—
it is only for the worst part of my condition that it is taken
up as my destiny. Existing demands of me the huge sacrifice of having no power, I desist and, behold, the world fits
in my weak hand. I desist and to my human poverty there
opens the only joy that is given me to have, human joy. I
know this and I tremble—living leaves me so much in
wonder, living keeps me from going to sleep.

I reach the height from which I can fall, I choose, I
tremble, and I desist, and finally, devoting myself to my fall,
depersonalized, without a voice of my own, in the last analysis without myself—behold that everything I don't have is
mine. I desist and the less I am, the more alive, the more I
lose my name, the more I am called, my only secret mission is my condition, I desist and the more I am ignorant of
the password the more I carry out the secret, the less I know
the more the sweetness of the abyss is my destiny. And then
I adore.

With my hands quietly folded in my lap, I was experiencing a sense of tender, timid happiness. It was almost a
nothingness, like when the breeze makes a blade of grass

quiver. It was almost nothing, but I could see the tiny movement of my timidity. I don't know, but I was approaching something with anguished idolatry and with the delicacy of one who fears. I was approaching the strongest thing that had yet happened to me.

Stronger than hope, stronger than love?

I was appoaching what I think was . . . confidence. Perhaps that's its name. Or it doesn't matter: you could give another one just as well.

I felt that my face was smiling in sweat. Or perhaps it wasn't smiling, I don't know. I was confident.

In myself? in the world? in God? in the cockroach? I don't know. Perhaps having confidence doesn't involve having it in something or someone. Perhaps I now knew that I would never be equal to life myself, but that my life was equal to life. I would never reach my root, but my root did exist. I had timidly let myself be transfixed by a sweetness that abashed me without constraining me.

Oh God, I felt baptized by the world. I had put cockroach matter into my mouth; I had finally performed the lowest of all acts.

Not the greatest of all acts as I had thought before, not heroism and sainthood. But in the final analysis, the lowest of all acts was what I had always needed. I had always been incapable of the lowest of acts. And like that lowest of acts, I had deheroized myself. I, who had lived of the middle of the road, had finally taken the first step at its start.

Finally, finally, my husk had really broken, and I was, without limit. By not being, I was. To the edge of what I wasn't, I was. What I am not, I am. Everything will be within me, if I am not; for "I" is merely one of the world's instantaneous spasms. My life doesn't have a merely human sense, it is much greater—it is so much greater that, in relation to human sense, it is senseless. Of the general organization that was greater than I, I had till now perceived only the fragments. But now I was much less than human . . . and I would realize my specifically human destiny only if I gave myself over, just as I was doing, to what was not me, to what was still inhuman.

And giving myself over with the confidence of belonging to the unknown. For I can pray only to what I do not know. And I can love only the unknown evidence of things and can add myself only to what I do not know. Only that is a real giving of oneself.

And such a giving of myself is the only surpassing that doesn't exclude me. I was now so much greater that I no longer saw myself. As great as a landscape in the distance. I was in the distance. More perceptible in my last mountains and in my remotest rivers: simultaneous nowness did not frighten me anymore, and in the most ultimate extremity of myself I could finally smile without smiling in the least. I finally extended beyond my own sensibility.

The world interdepended with me—that was the confidence I had reached: the world interdepended with me, and I am not understanding what I say, never! never again shall I understand what I say. For how will I be able to speak without the word lying for me? how will I be able to speak except timidly, like this: life is itself for me. Life is itself for me, and I don't understand what I am saying. And, therefore, I adore . . .

Clarice
LISPECTOR

Clarice Lispector, one of the most significant writers in twentieth-century Brazilian literature, died in 1977. Her works range from literary essays to novelistic fiction and children's literature. Lispector is best known in Latin America and Europe; only recently have some of her works been translated from Portuguese into English. Other English translations include *Family Ties*, *The Apple in the Dark* and *The Hour of the Star*. The University of Minnesota Press will soon publish a translation of her book *Agua Viva*.

Ronald Sousa, a faculty member at the University of Minnesota since 1974, is professor of Spanish and Portuguese and previously served as department chairman of comparative literature. He has also worked at the University of Texas and the University of California, Berkeley. Sousa received his master's degree (1968) and doctorate (1973) in comparative literature at the University of California, Berkeley. He is author of *The Rediscoverers: Major Figures in the Portuguese Literature of National Regeneration* and editor of *Problems of Enlightenment in Portugal*. Sousa contributes to *Ideologies and Literature*, *Luso-Brazilian Review* and *Bulletin of Hispanic Studies*.